KRAKOW

BY
SCOTT SIMPSON

Produced by
Thomas Cook Publishing

Written by Scott Simpson
Updated by Helena Zukowski
Original photography by Simon Cygielski
Updated photography by Christopher Holt
Original design by Laburnum
Technologies Pvt Ltd

Editing and page layout by Cambridge
Publishing Management Ltd, Unit 2,
Burr Elm Court, Caldecote CB3 7NU
Series Editor: Karen Beaulah

Published by Thomas Cook Publishing
A division of Thomas Cook Tour Operations Ltd

PO Box 227, The Thomas Cook Business Park,
Units 15–16, Coningsby Road, Peterborough PE3 8SB, United Kingdom
E-mail: books@thomascook.com
www.thomascookpublishing.com
Tel: +44 (0) 1733 416477

ISBN-13: 978-1-84157-573-5
ISBN-10: 1-84157-573-9

Text © 2006 Thomas Cook Publishing
Maps © 2006 Thomas Cook Publishing
First edition © 2003 Thomas Cook Publishing
Second edition © 2006 Thomas Cook Publishing

Project Editor: Linda Bass
Production/DTP Editor: Steven Collins

Printed and bound in Spain by: Grafo Industrias Gráficas, Basauri.

Cover design by: Liz Lyons Design, Oxford.
Front cover credits: Left © Petr Svarc/Alamy; centre © Robert Harding World Imagery/Alamy;
right © Krzysztof Dydynski/Getty
Back cover credits: Left © Kevin Foy/Alamy; right © Les Polders/Alamy

Contents

KEY TO MAPS
✈ Airport
★ Start of walk/tour
+++ Railway line
(780) Road number
✳ Viewpoint

Introduction

Cracovia totius Poloniae urbs celeberrima atque amplissima – 'Krakow is the most celebrated and greatest of all Polish cities' – wrote Matthew Merian of Amsterdam on his 1619 engraving of Krakow. Although no longer the capital of Poland, Krakow is arguably still the best known and most eagerly visited of Polish cities.

By the 7th or 8th century AD, the Wiślan tribe of the Slavs had settled in the swampy upper Wisła (Vistula) valley. Until Prince Mieszko of the neighbouring Polan (literally 'field-dwellers') tribe conquered the region about 988, the fortified town of Krakow was closely linked with the territories of Bohemia and Moravia to the south.

King Kazimierz (Casimir) I the Restorer moved the royal court of the infant Polish kingdom to Krakow in 1038 and Krakow enjoyed a golden age of growth. By the time of Kazimierz III the Great (ruled 1333–70) the city had expanded far beyond the ancient earthworks, and stone walls now girded it. The city was bracketed by two satellite towns, Kleparz and Kazimierz (named after its founder). Most importantly, the king founded a university, whose fate was inextricably entwined with the city's.

Krakow basked in the warmth of royal patronage until 28 May 1609 when Zygmunt (Sigismund) III and his court left Wawel, never to return. Warsaw became the capital, although kings and queens still made the journey to Krakow for their coronations and funerals in Wawel's cathedral.

Krakow was the cosmopolitan capital of a multi-ethnic kingdom. The streets were filled with Poles, Germans, Jews, Hungarians, Scots, Czechs, Walloons and Italians. When Krakow was annexed in 1795 to that vast portfolio of international real estate, the Habsburg Empire, Cracovians adapted with far more ease than other cities. Even today, Krakow fondly remembers the last emperor, Franz Joseph – his portrait may still be seen in many bars and cafés.

St Stanislaus' Cathedral

The Second World War marked the end of ethnic diversity, and the new communist government fought bitterly against Krakow's bourgeois values and entrenched Roman Catholicism. Cracovians remained stubbornly proud of their history and legends, devoted to cultured and sometimes overblown intellectual pursuits, and ostentatious in their allegiance to the Church. The new suburb of Nowa Huta was meant to give Krakow a proletarian slant, but it brought only steelworkers' strikes.

The election of Krakow's archbishop as Pope John Paul II in 1978 was one of the harbingers of the 'fall' of communism at the close of the 1980s. By the early 1990s, cafés and restaurants were appearing on every street, churches and palaces were being renovated and visitors from abroad had begun to rediscover one of Europe's most enchanting cities.

The magic and mystery of Krakow lurks in every brick of its Gothic mansions, in the echoing halls of its ancient Jagiellonian University, in the empty spaces of its synagogues. It is in the mist that rises from the Błonia fields in the morning and the peculiar quality of moonlight over its cobblestone streets. It is in the whispering murmur of the Vistula river and the secret silence of its limestone cliffs.

There is much to admire in Krakow's architecture

The City

To the north of Krakow lies the Great European Plain. It has been both a blessing and curse to Poland, being the easiest route east–west across the continent for traders but also for armies. Just north of the city lies the 'Krakow Gate', a pass through the foothills, and to the south lies the 'Moravian Gate', the easiest north–south passage through the Carpathian Mountains for hundreds of miles.

Kościół Mariacki

The Polish lands also mark out an intellectual borderland. This region fell just outside both the ancient Roman Empire and the medieval Carolingian Empire and yet it profited from cultural contact and trade with both. Along with Czech, Slovak, Slovenian and Croatian, Polish is one of the Slavic languages written with a Roman script. Poland is at the eastern edge of Western Christendom; going east from Krakow the countryside is increasingly dotted with Uniate and Orthodox churches as one nears the Ukrainian border. Krakow is home to the second-oldest university 'east of the Rhine and north of the Alps'. For travellers more used to the western parts of the continent, Central Europe will bring sudden flashes of recognition but also moments of bewildering strangeness.

Areas of Krakow

The heart of Krakow is the Old Town, laid out in 1257 and given encircling stone walls by Kazimierz the Great. It is shaped like a teardrop with the point facing south and the drip running north to Warsaw. Inside this citadel, you can still make out the outlines of the oldest

settlements of Krakow, the irregular streets of Okół around ul. Grodzka and the ramparts of the Wawel Hill. Set around Old Town, like numbers on a clock face, are districts that were once satellites, some legally quite separate.

At '12' on the clock face is Kleparz, founded in 1366 just north of Krakow's walls and incorporated into the city only in 1791. Built on the important north–south trade route, Kleparz is now home to two important outdoor vegetable markets.

The district east of Old Town is *Wesoła* (Joyous), with a large complex of hospital buildings and the Botanical Gardens. Much further out in this direction is the communist-built workers' town of *Nowa Huta* (New Forge), which partially overlays the medieval town of *Mogiła* (Burial Mound).

Stradom, founded in 1335, lies to the south. Historically, it was a suburb of Kazimierz, which was then an island connected to Stradom only by the *Pons Regalis* (Royal Bridge). This branch of the Wisła has since been filled in, but the river still flows on the other side of Kazimierz, setting it apart from

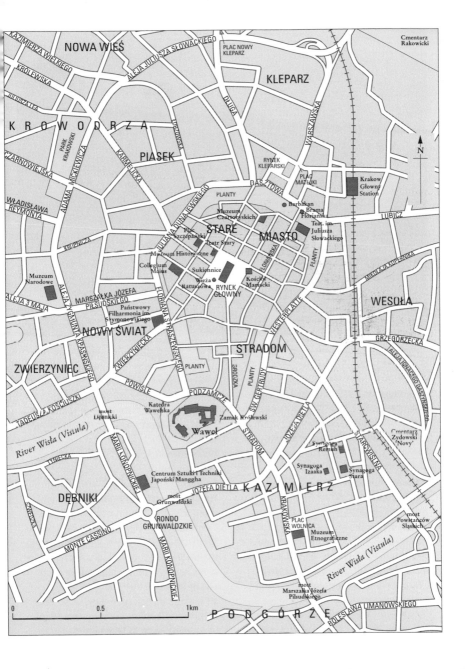

Krak's Mound overlooking Podgórze

Podgórze (Under Hill). Podgórze was declared an imperial city in 1784 by Emperor Joseph II and, for a brief period in the 19th century, it also lay on the far side of an international border between the Free City of Krakow and the Habsburg Empire. Kazimierz too became part of Krakow in 1791.

On the far side of the river, but further west, lies the sleepy district of Dębniki where the late Pope John Paul II lived as a poor student. On the north bank of the river facing Dębniki is the old settlement of Zwierzyniec, with three intriguing churches and the 'Garden City' of Salwator.

Northwest of Old Town, the sandy suburb of Piasek with its old Carmelite monastery has been engulfed by Krakow. Further out, the village of Czarna Wieś (Black Village) once boasted rich black earth, which provided the royal kitchens with vegetables. Today, that soil is hidden under Krakow's cityscape.

Climate

Krakow's climate is caught between three weather patterns: the warm Gulf currents from more southerly reaches of the Atlantic, the stormy wet winds from the Baltic and the cold, dry Arctic winds from the northeast. The weather tends to swing between these very different patterns, sometimes in the course of a single day. Always prepare for a range of temperatures. Winters are damp and dark. The average temperature in January in Krakow is 0°C (32°F) but there are intermittent snaps as low as –15°C (5°F). Summers are warm and dry with sudden flares of very hot weather. The average temperature in June and July in Krakow is 21°C (70°F) but it might rise to 30°C (86°F). Smog and inversion in Krakow's valley can be suffocating in the hottest weather.

It pays to be prepared for a sharp shower

History

c. 50,000 BC	First known settlement on Wawel Hill: remains of a flint-chipping workshop.
6th–7th centuries AD	Slavic tribes filter into Krakow region, replacing Celtic and Germanic cultures.
7th–8th centuries AD	Time of the legendary King Krak and his daughter, Queen Wanda, and probable date of Krak's Mound. Krakow is an important stronghold of the Wiślan tribe with close ties to Moravia in the south.

Monument to the Battle of Grunwald (1410)

965	First written record of Krakow, by Ibrahim ibn Jakub, a Jewish merchant from the Iberian peninsula. Krakow now an important settlement under the Bohemian (Czech) crown.
c. 998	Krakow and the Wiślan lands conquered by Prince Mieszko of the Polan tribe and become the embryo of the Polish state.
1038	Kazimierz (Casimir) I the Restorer moves Polish court from Gniezno in Wielkopolska (Greater Poland), its traditional home, to Krakow in Małopolska (Lesser Poland).
1079	Bishop Stanisław (Stanislaus) of Szczepanowo executed by King Bolesław II the Bold. Stanisław was later made a saint and the king was forced to flee to Hungary.
1241	Townspeople take refuge in Kościoł św. Andrzeja (St Andrew's Church) when Tartar horsemen from Central Asia pillage the city. Legendary origin of *hejnał* (dawn) bugle call.

1257

Krakow receives town law. Rynek Główny laid out and new walls also embrace sizeable Jewish community.

1335

Town status granted to Kazimierz, which engulfs the older settlements of Skałka (Cliff) and Bawół, on an island in the river.

1364

Founding of Academia Cracoviensis, later the Jagiellonian University. 'Summit of Kings' brings six monarchs to a sumptuous feast hosted by a citizen named Wierzynek.

1370

Death of Kazimierz (Casimir) III the Great ends Piast Dynasty, and Ludwik the Hungarian rushes to Krakow to claim the throne, but then rules from Visegrád, near Budapest. Poland under regency of Queen Elżbieta and, without royal patronage, Academia Cracoviensis goes into sharp decline.

1400

Lithuanian King Jagiełło buys large building (part of Collegium Maius) in the Jewish Quarter for the refounded university, later renamed 'Jagiellonian University' in his honour.

Money comes from a bequest of gold and jewels by his wife Jadwiga (*d*. 1399).

1491–5

Mikołaj Kopernik (Nicolaus Copernicus) of Toruń studies in Krakow. His astronomical instruments are preserved in the Jagiellonian University Museum.

1609

Zygmunt (Sigismund) III moves Polish court to Warsaw. New building slows down, preserving the medieval character of the city.

The 'Royal Route' through Krakow Old Town

General Tadeusz Kościuszko

1772   First Partition chops off a third of Poland and divides it between Prussia, Russia and Habsburg Empire (Austria).

1775   M. Sędrakowski opens first café in Krakow at Rynek Główny 31.

1793   Poland gets a liberal constitution, supported by King Stanisław Augustus. In response, Russia and Prussia invade to carve off new slices of Polish land.

1795   In spite of a daring insurrection to regain the lost territories by General Tadeusz Kościuszko, hero of the War of American Independence, Krakow becomes part of Habsburg Empire in Third (and final) Partition. Stanisław Augustus forced to abdicate and Poland ceases to exist as an independent country.

1810–14   Krakow's fortifications are levelled and Planty gardens are laid out in their place.

1815–46   Republic of Krakow, also known as Free City of Krakow, is created as a puppet state, dominated by Habsburg Empire.

1878–80   Swamp-clogged Stara Wisła (Old Vistula) branch of river filled in. Island of Kazimierz is physically joined to the rest of Krakow.

1918   Poland regains her independence, legalised by the Treaty of Versailles in 1919.

1926–35   Military dictatorship of Marshal Józef Piłsudski. He is buried in a crypt near the kings of Poland on Wawel Hill.

1939   On 1 September, German
aeroplanes bombard
Krakow and Nazi forces
take the city five days
later. On 6 November,
Krakow's university
professors are arrested in
Sonderaktion Krakau and
deported to concentration
camps.

1941   Jewish Ghetto created in
Podgórze. At its peak
containing 20,000 people,
it is liquidated on 13–14
March 1943.

1945   Krakow liberated by
Soviet forces. In the 1946
'People's Referendum'
Krakow votes against
communism, which takes
hold anyway and the city
is branded 'reactionary'.

1949   Building begins on
workers' planned suburb
of Nowa Huta.

1978   Archbishop of Krakow,
Karol Wojtyła, becomes
Pope John Paul II.

1980   Solidarność (Solidarity
trade union) founded
with Lech Wałęsa, an
unemployed electrician
from Gdańsk, as
chairman.

1981–3   Under the threat of Soviet
invasion, General

Wojciech Jaruzelski
declares Martial Law.
It lasts until 1983 but
economy continues
downward spiral until
end of 1980s.

1989   Solidarity negotiates
democratic elections at
the 'Round Table' talks
and proceeds to win
control of government.
Tadeusz Mazowiecki, a
journalist, becomes first
non-communist Prime
Minister in the post-war
Eastern Bloc.

1999   Poland joins NATO.

2004   Poland joins the EU
1 March 2004.

2005   Pope John Paul II
dies on 2 April.

Solidarity

Limestone and Marsh

Medieval travellers from three directions had to traverse river, marsh or swamp to reach the high ground of Krakow. Only the well-guarded northern approach along the trade route to Toruń was across dry land.

The natural defences of swamps, ponds and rivers guarded Krakow well for hundreds of years. The king's castle occupied a vantage point on the limestone cliffs of Wawel and townspeople sheltered below in the fortified ring of Okół (the Circle).

The largest swamp was called Żabi Kruk (literally 'frog's raven'), a rather poetic name for the great cormorant, a black, marsh bird – now an endangered species in Poland. Several small rivers – the Wilga (Golden Oriole), Rudawa (Ruddy-Coloured) and Prądnik (Little Current) – ran down from the hills, through these swamps and into the Wisła (Vistula) river near the bend that wrapped around the Wawel (probably an old Slavic word for 'dry spot in a swamp'), only to be broken into two currents by Skała (Cliff). The wider branch cut off Skała's island (now Kazimierz) from the rest of Krakow and was called Stara Wisła (Old Vistula).

Behind the sheltering rock of Wawel, the wedge-shaped *Służek Prądnika* (Prądnik Plateau) spread northward. It was an inviting place to settle, if less easily defended than the limestone outcrops. The oldest portion of Krakow, Okół, stayed close to the sharp point of the plateau and defended the open northern perimeter with a moat and earthworks.

As Krakow expanded beyond the safety of the rocks and plateaux, the wetlands were filled in for settlement. Today, the ghosts of long-gone waterways lurk in the place names of Krakow. The Stara Wisła river is gone but ul. Starowiślna still crosses its dry banks. Plac Na Groblach (Square on the Fishponds) under Wawel is now filled with a sports centre without a pond or fish in sight. Likewise, no modern stream runs near ul. Dolnych Młynów (Lower Watermills).

When wandering through Krakow's streets, you can often guess the original lie of the land by looking at the age of the buildings. Streets with several old buildings clustered together represent the high ground; districts with row upon row of 20th-century buildings are the old swamps. The most radical change to Krakow's topography was the filling in of the Stara Wisła in 1878–80. Building had considerably changed the water table and the river had become clogged and swampy. The old riverbed now lies under ul. Dietla.

Opposite: Marshy banks of Wisła (Vistula) south of Krakow
Above: The walls of Wawel Hill rise from the river

Governance

As they say about themselves, 'Two Poles, three opinions'. The contentious nature of its politicians served Poland well when Poles were united to cast off foreign occupation. However, in the absence of a clear common enemy, infighting has often weakened the health of the nation.

Krakow's Town Hall

Freedom regained and the inter-war period

After nearly two centuries of being divided among three neighbouring powers, Poland miraculously reappeared in the power vacuum at the messy end of the First World War. Austria and Germany were defeated and Russia was in the throes of the Communist Revolution. In 1918, Commander-in-Chief Józef Piłsudski (1867–1935) persuaded what remained of the occupying powers to abandon Polish territory. Within a year, the Treaty of Versailles confirmed Poland's renewed status as a sovereign state. Among the first of the nation's Prime Ministers was Ignacy Paderewski, the renowned pianist.

Euphoria was short-lived as several short wars, divisive politics and the economic effects of the 'Great Slump' took the shine off independence. The first constitutionally elected President, Gabriel Narutowicz (1865–1922), was assassinated five days after being sworn in as President and the politicians that followed seemed unable to control the chaos. In 1926, Piłsudski took power again in a military coup.

On 1 September 1939, the Nazi army smashed through Polish defences. In addition to being poorly equipped to fight a mechanised war, Polish military strategy mistakenly relied on promised help from British and French forces, which never came. The Nazis had taken control of Krakow by the end of the week.

With an eye to its cosmopolitan past, Krakow was declared to be a German city and Governor-General Hans Frank (1900–46) took up residence in Wawel Castle. In accordance with a secret agreement (the Molotov-Ribbentrop Pact) with the Nazis, the Soviet Army invaded the other half of Poland on 17 September. Poland ceased to exist again after only 21 years of freedom.

Communism and the People's Republic

Krakow was 'liberated' from the Nazis in January 1945 by the Soviet Army. Under Soviet control, Krakow was branded a reactionary and bourgeois city. To remedy this, the communist government built a huge industrial complex named Nowa Huta (New Forge) and a proletarian model city nearby.

In 1977, a student dissident at the Jagiellonian University, Stanisław Pyjas, was murdered by the secret police and his death clumsily covered up as suicide. The result was the 'Black March' from the site of the murder to Wawel, increased student agitation and a long-term worsening of relations between the intelligentsia of Krakow and the communist government.

Solidarność (the Solidarity trade union) was founded in 1980, uniting a broad coalition of dissidents. The movement drew much of its strength from the support of the Roman Catholic Church, it acquired sound strategy and contacts abroad from the intelligentsia, and won over the masses with the charisma of Solidarity's leader, Lech Wałęsa, an electrician from Gdańsk with a working-class accent.

Developments in Poland threatened Soviet hegemony in the region. By winter of 1981, many expected an invasion of Soviet Bloc troops, like that which crushed the Prague Spring in 1968. In a move that remains controversial, General Wojciech Jaruzelski (1923–) pre-empted invasion by declaring Martial Law. It lasted until 1983.

Post-communist Poland

Solidarity's 'Round Table' negotiations with Jaruzelski's government in 1989 resulted in free elections, which Solidarity won. Tadeusz Mazowiecki, a journalist, became the first non-communist Prime Minister in the post-war Eastern Bloc.

The new government saw the start of a decade of turbulent growth, beginning inauspiciously with hyperinflation.

Groping attempts at a capitalist market were largely unregulated as thousands of little local businesses sprung up on the streets and big international corporations opened branches. The Warsaw Stock Exchange (WSE) was established in 1991 and the currency was re-valued in 1995, slicing off now-useless zeros.

Democratic elections were a novelty to most Poles. Impossible campaign promises and unknown candidates were taken seriously. The myriad parties were highly fragmented, and the 'Polish Friends of Beer' were the largest single party in the *Sejm* (Parliament) during one government.

Visitors who hope to see the 'wild east' of post-communist Europe today, however, are likely to be disappointed. The boom of the 1990s has passed and politics are increasingly stabilised. As one financial analyst recently remarked, 'Poland is turning out to be a rather normal European country', though serious problems remain in Poland's large agricultural sector and under-funded public services like health and education.

Poland joined NATO in 1999 and the European Union (EU) in 2004.

Election poster

Culture

Krakow prides itself on its sobriquet 'the Cultural Capital of Poland', often looking down on what Cracovians see as Warsaw's vulgar obsession with money and political power. As the poet Sikorowski wrote 'Don't bring the capital back to Krakow!'

Unburdened of its role as royal capital and with its significance as a trade centre greatly reduced, Krakow's identity has become bound up in its self-perception as a city of painters, poets and musicians. Small galleries are a common sight on Krakow's streets and many bars and cafés host

Music on the streets, Krakow style

exhibits. If conversation in Warsaw often revolves around who will be signing a business deal soon, in Krakow it often turns on who will be exhibiting their artwork soon.

Art and architecture
Of the ancient art of the Slavic people, little survives. The famous Światowid of Zbrucz in the Archaeological Museum is one of the few pieces of significance from the pre-Christian era.

Western Christianity brought with it new art forms. The Romanesque style was borrowed from the Germanic Holy Roman Empire of Otto III and his successors. One of the best examples is the crypt of St Leonard under the Wawel Cathedral, but many other Krakow churches in later styles also hide a Romanesque crypt. These churches pre-date the strict

CHANGES

Although the spirit of Krakow may seem immutable, the particulars change often. New cafés open and old ones close at an amazing rate. Renovation of many buildings continues, leading to unexpected closures at inconvenient moments. Famous works of art sometimes go on loan to other museums. Furthermore, it is an established Krakow tradition that opening hours should follow complicated formulae, containing phrases like 'closed every third Sunday', making your Sunday visit into a kind of tourist roulette. If that were not enough, opening hours usually change from season to season, without advance notice. (The opening hours listed in this guide were correct at the time of writing.)

grid pattern of streets and are often at odd angles to the buildings around them.

New vogues in art travelled quickly along the trade routes. Keeping up with western neighbours in patronage of the arts was an important part of royal propaganda. Gothic architecture arrived with monastic orders such as the Cistercians, and was soon copied by the Dominicans and Franciscans. This new style flourished, especially under Kazimierz the Great. Three of the largest churches in Krakow (Kościół Mariacki, św. Katarzyna, Bożego Ciała) were built or rebuilt with his patronage and are examples of the soaring grace of Gothic

The Crypt of St Leonard under Wawel Cathedral

architecture, in Krakow's typical brick and limestone.

The Renaissance arrived just in time for Poland's 'Golden Age' and prosperity allowed many noble families to build ostentatious palaces and rich tombs. The style is especially well represented in the Royal Castle and also in the buildings around it on Wawel Hill.

The Baroque was another style that rode into Poland on the shoulders of a religious order, this time the Jesuits. The style was imported from Italy, either directly (as with Matteo Castelli's faithful copy of the Roman Il Gesú in Kościół św. Piotra i Pawła, completed in 1630) or via Moravia (as was Kacper Bażanek's Kościół Pijarów, completed in 1728).

Poland's most original contributions to European art came with the Young Poland movement, a local style associated with Art Nouveau. This burst of creativity attempted to unify all the arts and crafts into a seamless whole: not only architecture, sculpture, painting, furniture and stained glass but also theatre and poetry. Wyspiański's bold reinterpretation of the Gothic interior of the Franciscan Church is an outstanding example.

The massive Modernist buildings (such as the Main Branch of the National Museum) erected by the inter-war governments can be hard to tell apart from early forms of the Socialist Realism imposed by Soviet doctrine. In its final days, Socialist Realism sometimes lurched into quirky Post-Modernism, like the bulky Hotel Forum perched up on stilts.

Images of Krakow

The painter Jan Matejko (1838–93) devoted his entire career to recreating Poland's history. His canvases were often vast, wall-sized scenes, painted in excruciating detail showing crucial moments in history. One of his most famous is *Hołd Pruski* (the *Prussian Oath of Fealty*), which can be viewed in the gallery above the Sukiennice. It depicts an event that took place in 1525 – only 30m (100ft) from where the painting hangs (the building can be seen in the background of the painting) – when the last Grand Master of the Teutonic Knights paid homage to Zygmunt I the Old. Matejko was also responsible for the renovated polychrome adorning the walls of Kościół Mariacki.

One of the many events at the Philharmonic

The Krakow skyline features in many paintings

Matejko's student, Stanisław Wyspiański (1869–1907), was the brightest star of the Young Poland movement. He focused on the Krakow of his own day, capturing views of the Kopiec Kościuszki and the Błonia fields from the window of his studio. Wyspiański's plan to remake the Wawel Hill (1906) as the 'Acropolis' of Krakow – with a theatre, a stadium, a national museum and schools – was drawn up while Austro-Hungarian troops were still using the hill as their headquarters and barracks.

Music

When the Nazis took control of Krakow in 1939, they closed the Academy of Music, forbade Poles to attend the German-only opera and outlawed Chopin's music in any form. Cracovians continued to hold concerts in private homes, risking imprisonment for the sake of Polish music. Within two months of Krakow's liberation in 1945, the Philharmonic was giving public concerts again, along with many excellent musicians who had escaped the destruction of Warsaw.

Krzysztof Penderecki (1933–) is one of the giants of modern serious music, famous for his unnerving, restless orchestral and choral pieces of the 1970s – his more recent works are more mellowed with a hint of neo-Romanticism. His surrealist opera *Król Ubu*, based on Jarry's *Ubu Rex*, is sometimes performed in Krakow's Opera and his orchestral works are part of the Philharmonic's repertoire.

Zbigniew Preisner (1955–) is best known for his award-winning film scores in Poland, France and Hollywood. A memorable example is the central tune that haunts Kieślowski's *Double Life of Veronica* about two women leading strangely parallel lives in Paris and Krakow. His album *Preisner's Music* (internationally available) features many of his more famous compositions, recorded at a concert deep inside the Wieliczka salt mines.

Catch a live performance while you are in town

Bookshops abound in bookish Krakow

Literature and drama

One of the more strangely successful attempts to stimulate artists to greater creativity under communism was the Dom Literatów (Writer's House) on ul. Krupnicza. It was a state-sponsored artist colony in an urban setting. Writers of all genres and dispositions were tossed together in a dormitory with a library and a dining hall. They often arrived with families, lovers or secretaries in tow. Among the most famous long-term inhabitants were the humorist, Mrożek, and the Nobel prize-winning poet, Szymborska. This curious hothouse of talent, unfortunately, could not survive the rough winds of the 1980s and withered away.

One frequent visitor to the Dom Literatów was Stanisław Lem (1921–), Poland's most famous science-fiction writer. Born in Lviv in what is now Ukraine (but was then Poland) his medical studies were interrupted by the Second World War. He came to Krakow after the war to finish his degree at the Jagiellonian University but achieved his greatest success as a writer. His novel *Solaris* has twice been filmed (the Russian classic by Tarkovsky and recently by Hollywood). More ambitious than many sci-fi authors, Lem delves into questions of memory, identity and epistemology. His books are available in many languages, including English. An asteroid was named after Lem in 1992.

Another Polish author whose place of birth is no longer in Poland but who has found a second home in Krakow is Czesław Miłosz (1911–2004). Born in what is now Lithuania, Miłosz spent many years in exile in France and the USA before returning to Poland. He settled in Krakow because it reminded him of old Vilnius. In 1980, Miłosz won the Nobel Prize for literature. Many of Miłosz's books, especially his *History of Polish Literature*, are easily available in English.

For such a small city, it is unusual that Krakow can boast two poets with Nobel Prizes in literature. Wisława Szymborska (1923–) won the prize in 1996, suddenly bringing her to international attention. Although her early work had been very much in the state-approved aesthetic of praise for progress, over time she developed laconic but intimate poems on the existential problems of human existence. Her *view with a grain of sand* is available in English.

Krakow's many theatres have kept playwrights and directors busy. One closely associated with Krakow was Tadeusz Kantor (1915–90). After organising illegal theatre performances under Nazi occupation, Kantor went on to become communist Poland's foremost avant-garde theatre director and designer. His performances often pushed the boundaries between theatre and unbridled performance art using both real actors and lifeless mannikins, abstract sets, snatches of songs, tableaux and processions. His masterpiece *Umarła Klasa* (*The Dead Class*) is more often praised than performed these days.

Although Andrzej Wajda (1926–) has directed stage plays in Krakow's prestigious Stary Teatr, he is best known as a film director, adapting Polish literary classics for the screen. His semi-fictional portrayals of social unrest in Poland in *Man of Marble* (1976) and *Man of Iron* (1981) were important pieces of image-building abroad for the young Solidarity movement. In 1994, Wajda donated money that he had received from a Japanese film competition to build the 'Manggha' centre to promote Japanese art in Krakow. In 2000, he received an Oscar for lifetime achievement.

Wisława Szymborska's Nobel Prize-winning poetry

Impressions

Ale Kraków jest mały! 'Krakow is so small!' Cracovians love to exclaim when bumping into a friend or co-worker unexpectedly. Its population is nearly 900,000 but, somehow, everyone seems to know everyone else.

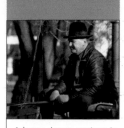

A horse-drawn carriage in Old Town

Krakow is a walking city. Cars have difficulty with its cobblestones and narrow streets and public transport does not run through much of Old Town: travel by foot is easiest. The soothing greenery of the Planty gardens lets you take a quiet stroll at a leisurely pace. The bustle of Rynek Główny is the place to promenade in order to see and be seen.

The city spreads out in concentric rings of age. The oldest buildings cluster together on the high ground; newer buildings stand on successively lower ground. Those of interest to visitors are naturally grouped together. The most famous, of course, are well marked and

Summer in Krakow

surrounded by shops selling souvenirs, but there are other clusters of old and beautiful buildings that do not get as much tourist traffic. Wandering off the beaten path is often a very rewarding experience. Krakow is a very open and accessible city to visitors, partly because of the many students who come to study at its universities and the increasing number of tourists.

When to go

Late May and early June are usually sunny, green and leafy, often the most pleasant weather of the year. Many festivals and outdoor events take advantage of this window. The middle part of summer in Krakow is usually hot, often leading to atmospheric inversion and smog in Krakow's valley. Many Cracovians escape to the mountains or seaside for the muggy months of July and August. Things cool down in September and early October, which are also attractive times to travel to Krakow. However, late autumn, winter and early spring are cold, dark, wet and prone to sudden snaps below zero.

Most hotels charge more in June, July and August. Hotel reservations in summer can be difficult because of tour groups blocking out rooms in the larger hotels.

Remember that Poles tend to spend religious holidays with their family. Many shops, bars and museums are closed around Easter and Christmas, even on days that aren't official state holidays. Travel within Poland can be difficult then: public transport is reduced but the number of people rushing home to their families is increased.

Getting around

The main sights of Krakow are in the compact Old Town, where walking is almost always the easiest way to get between two points. Public transport runs around the edge of Old Town and out into the suburbs. It is easy to use and cheap.

Trams

There are 518 tramcars running along Krakow's 286km (178 miles) of tracks. On many routes, they run about every 15 minutes during the day. During rush hours when the roads clog up, trams run relatively unhindered. There are convenient tram routes from the centre to most of the outlying sights, including the 1, 2 and 6 to Salwator. Major investment is currently being made in the transport system, with tram lines being extended and new trams purchased. The project is scheduled to finish in 2008.

Buses

There are 516 city buses on Krakow's 1,497km (935 miles) of bus routes. Municipal buses run much further out

Krakow Environs

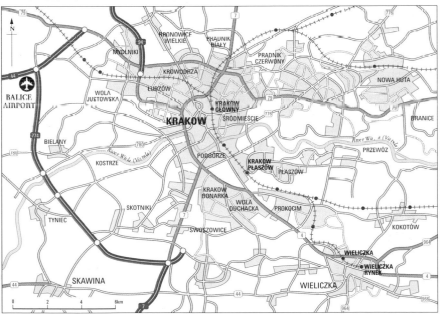

than trams, sometimes to the nearer villages. Buses also run into some of the larger parks and are the easiest way to get to the zoo and Kopiec Kościuszki. There are night buses after 11pm.

Taxis

Most taxis are quite cheap compared to Western Europe but it is best to stick to those in one of the tele-taxi associations. These can be recognised by the telephone number prominently displayed on the roof or sides of the taxi. If you have called a taxi, rather than hailing one on the street, you should pay slightly less than the sum on the meter: ask your driver for the correct amount. You may ask for a receipt and this is recommended if you suspect that you have been overcharged.

Avoid the taxis that prowl around the railway station. The taxi rank at the airport with '919' taxis is safe.

Trams are cheap and easy to use

Car

Most visitors do not find that driving their own car in Krakow is convenient. Krakow's complicated zone system, marking which streets may be used for what purpose by which people at what hours, is almost impossible for outsiders to master. The driving style is aggressive and erratic, with frequent sudden stops as pedestrians blithely cross the street in unexpected places. Car parks are scarce and visitors often find clamps on their vehicles because of parking violations that they did not understand. It is much more convenient to leave vehicles at the hotel and take public transport or walk.

Pollution

Krakow lies in a valley with the high-pollution region of Silesia to the west and the steel mills of Nowa Huta to the east. Although pollution is no longer at the horrifying levels of the 1980s, Krakow's air is still dirty. Health warnings are sometimes issued in newspapers about air quality and Krakow's monuments require additional protection from acid rain.

Ironically, the failure of many large Silesian factories has been greatly beneficial in reducing pollution in the region. As production was cut back at the steelworks in Nowa Huta, the oldest units were retired first, leaving only newer and more efficient units in use.

Many Cracovians still heat their homes in winter on cheap, brown coal. At the start of cold weather, Krakow is often wreathed in a blue haze of coal-smoke. The smell sticks to clothes and carries for many miles. Some visitors, especially the elderly, may notice a

The cobblestone streets of Krakow

slight increase in respiratory problems during the hottest and coldest months of the year.

Recycling programmes are popular with Krakow's residents. Most hotels, however, do not have separate bins for recyclables. Glass, paper and plastic bottles may be deposited in the brightly-coloured domes for recycling. Recycling domes are more common in the residential areas, rarer in the tourist areas.

Manners and mores

Krakow is very public about its religious observance. You may find even very tough-looking youths making the sign of the cross when passing a church or roadside shrine. Poles are traditionally very respectful towards the elderly – who are not afraid to demand preferential treatment. If you fail to give your seat to an older passenger on a crowded tram or bus, you will be summarily glared at. Little old ladies also tend to act as if rules about pedestrian crossings do not apply to them.

When sitting down to a meal together, Poles always wish each other *Smacznego!* ('*Bon appetit*') even if they are complete strangers. When entering someone's home, remove your shoes once you are through the door (they will probably offer you slippers); it is recommended that you bring a gift of flowers or a bottle of wine.

When entering a shop, many Cracovians still say *dzień dobry* (hello) to the shopkeeper and *do widzenie* (goodbye) or *dziękuję* (thank you) when leaving. Clients and customers always address each other with the formal *Pan* (Mr/Sir) or *Pani* (Ms/Ma'am). Unfortunately, this ritual observance does not always translate into good customer service.

In spite of the omnipresent Roman Catholic Church, Cracovians of both sexes flirt more often than residents of Anglo-Saxon countries. Be aware that such flirting may be quite innocent and is part of the local means of communication. Women in Poland are more likely to hold positions of power in business or government than in many Western countries but at the same time they bear the burden of very traditional expectations in the home. Children are likely to be supported by their parents and live at home until their mid-twenties or even later.

Cost of living

In spite of steep inflation in the 1990s, Krakow remains very cheap for visitors. Most locally-produced goods and services are about half the price of their equivalents in Western Europe. Imported goods are, not surprisingly, a little more expensive than in their country of origin.

The Barbakan

Old Town

Krakow has been the seat of kings, archbishops, monks, magnates and merchants for a thousand years. Each generation has added treasures to the city, leaving the visitor with an embarrassment of cultural riches to explore. Visitors who are in Krakow for only a few days should concentrate on the famous sights of Old Town, Wawel and Wieliczka, but those who are lucky enough to tarry longer will find the less well-known nooks and crannies just as rewarding.

Barbakan

Mounted knights ceased to dominate European warfare in the 15th century and gunpowder weapons grew increasingly sophisticated. In 1498–9, with a Turkish invasion looming, King Jan I 'Olbracht' renovated Krakow's fortifications using the latest ideas. The masterpiece of his new defences was the beautiful and deadly late-Gothic barbican at the northern edge of the walls.

Krakow's barbican is the largest in Central Europe and one of the very few that have survived anywhere. Its red-brick walls are 3m (10ft) thick, with three galleries for small artillery, and pierced with 130 firing 'loops'. The barbican walls are topped by overhanging brickwork pierced by holes – 'machicolation' – through which defenders could shoot arrows and drop stones or hot liquid on to attackers. This massive fortification is topped by seven *bartizans*, small lookout turrets, with steep roofs. They did not really need seven, but Gothic architects were fond of mystical numbers.

The barbican was originally on an island between the two moats. You crossed a drawbridge over the outer moat and passed under a gateway into the courtyard of the barbican. From there a narrow, fortified bridge crossed the inner moat to the Floriańska Gate. If you tried to force your way through, you would find your path blocked by portcullises dropped from above. You were trapped and could then be shot at leisure from the battlements.

The barbican remained undefeated, even by the 1768 Russian attack, until the surrounding fortifications were removed in the 19th century. A plaque hangs on the wall in memory of tailor Marcin Oraczewski who, according to legend, when bullets ran out, loaded his musket with buttons and killed the Russian General. *Open: Apr–Oct, 10.30am–6pm.*

Brama Floriańska

For hundreds of years Brama Floriańska was the main gate to Krakow, guarding the open, northern approach to the city.

The first gate, of earthwork and wood, was raised at some time after 1285 as part of the defences for the new districts around Rynek Główny. It was replaced with a low, limestone tower in the 14th century. The upper storeys and their machicolated brickwork were added in the 15th century, together with the Barbican beyond the walls. The bronze crown on the tower dates from 1647.

The side of the tower that faces Old Town is decorated with a Baroque bas-relief showing St Florian, patron saint of fire brigades, putting out a burning town with a pitcher of water. The opposite side is adorned with a Polish eagle designed by the Historicist painter Matejko. Inside the gate is a small shrine to the Virgin Mary, moved there in 1835 from the walled bridge that once linked Brama Floriańska with the barbican.

The gate, walls and towers visible today are only a small fragment of the medieval defences. There were once 39 towers, eight main gates and several posterns. Outside the walls ran a double moat whose inner ring was in places 22m (72ft) wide and 8m (26ft) deep. The water came from the Rudawa river and emptied into the Wisła. The outer bank of the moats was kept clear of buildings, to deny cover to any invader.

In 1810 the Habsburg authorities began to level Krakow's fortifications. The short stretch of northern walls that contains Brama Floriańska was the last left standing and was in danger of being pulled down in 1817. Feliks Radwański (1756–1826), a Krakow

Brama Floriańska guards the northern approach to Old Town

A mask on the Sukiennice gable

architect, pointed out the historical importance of the gate, the opportunity to attract tourists and, last but not least, the terrible meteorological and health problems that might arise: cold northern winds would blow unchecked into Krakow and 'with regard to health, delicately bred women and children would be exposed to frequent gum disease, rheumatism and maybe even paralysis'. The city senate spared the walls.

The three towers that still stand on either side of the Floriańska Gate are the Pasamoników (Tailors'), Stolarska (Joiners') and Ciesielska (Carpenters') towers. Each was named after the guild that was assigned to maintain and defend it. Although Brama Floriańska is the only gate that remains open, the Butchers' Gate became part of the buildings of the Dominican Cloister and its remains can be seen from the Planty near ul. Mikołajska.

Mały Rynek

Long before the town planning of 1257 set out this square, there was a market here on the crossroads of two trade routes. Mały Rynek (the Small Market Square) was originally the Butchers' Market, filled with rows of stalls selling meat and fish. In the 18th century, it switched to vegetables and fruit. In 1903, the stalls were ejected to make room for tram tracks, which in turn were removed in 1953. It now serves as a car park in winter, a beer garden in summer. *Kamienicy* stand along three sides of the square. The fourth side is taken up by church buildings, notably the backs of Kościół Mariacki and Kościół św. Barbary.

Plac Mariacki

This is actually two small, quiet courtyards. Next to the bustle of the Rynek Główny, they were until 1796 the cemetery of the Mariacki church, whose bulk cuts the 'square' in two. The streets around follow the town plan of 1257. Kościół Mariacki, however, stands on the foundations of an earlier church and is at an angle.

The different colours of paving stones mark where the old walls and the five gates to the cemetery stood. Cracovian burghers were buried here until the new burial regulations in 1791. Funerary chapels line the outsides of Kościół Mariacki and Kościół św. Barbary, with memorial plaques in a variety of styles from the 16th to the 19th centuries.

The 15th-century Gothic cemetery chapel attached to Kościół św. Barbary, showing Jesus and three disciples, was probably executed by a pupil of Wit Stwosz. The fountain in the centre of the square – known as Pomnik Żaczka (the Student's Monument) – is a 1958 copy of a figure from Wit Stwosz's altar screen in Kościół Mariacki.

Although the main gate out into the Rynek Główny was torn down with the cemetery walls about 1796, the Baroque figure of the Merciful Mother of God that used to top the gate has survived. She now stands on a pillar at the end of ul. Jagiellońska. In one hand, she holds a sceptre of authority, in the other, the broken arrows of mercy.

Krakow legend states that the statue was funded by the mother of a soldier who was heavily wounded in the 1768 Russian attack and was mistakenly believed to be dead. He was buried in a mass grave in the Mariacki churchyard but when his mother prayed to the

Virgin Mary, she took pity on him and revived him. The soldier clawed his way out of the grave and into the arms of his grateful mother.

Plac św. Marii Magdaleny (St Mary Magdalene's Square)

This small square between ul. Grodzka and ul. Kanonicza dates from the days when most of 'Old Town' had not yet been built. This was the main square of the old settlement of Okoł (the Circle). A small church dedicated to Mary Magdalene stood here from the early 14th century until 1811. The northern edge of the square, where the market stalls stood in the 14th century, is now filled by Collegium Iuridicum (*see p96*). The two churches that dominate the Grodzka side of the square are a sharp contrast – Kościół św. Piotra i Pawła (Sts Peter and Paul's Church, *see p46*) is flamboyant Baroque while Kościół św. Andrzeja (St Andrew's Church, *see p40*) is one of Krakow's two oldest Romanesque churches. The square also contains a subtle contemporary fountain and a not-so-subtle monument to Piotr Skarga, a Jesuit preacher who lies buried in the church opposite.

Rynek Główny (The Main Market Square)

Rynek Główny is a spacious square surrounded by tall townhouses and palaces. The centre of the square is dominated by the Sukiennice (the Cloth Hall) and Wieża Ratuszowa (the Town Hall Tower) while the graceful Gothic towers of Kościół Mariacki (St Mary's Church, *see pp43–4*) soar over the entrance from ul. Floriańska. When

Rynek Główny

Looking for something that says 'Krakow'

older ul. Grodzka takes the place of two streets.

Originally filled with low market buildings, the Rynek gets its name from the ring road that ran around the market. The Sukiennice, which now stands in a largely empty square, was once flanked by rows of stalls and administrative buildings. On one side, the Wieża Ratuszowa is all that remains of a town hall that filled nearly a quarter of the square. On the other side, between Kościół św. Wojciecha and the Sukiennice were the Great and Lesser Scales, a guarantee that even traders from far-off lands were using the standard weights of the kingdom.

The outside of the ring also looked very different. The level of the square in the 13th and 14th centuries was about half a storey lower than today. Most *kamienice* had a broad porch in front, protected by a wooden roof and a railing. Stairs led half a storey up from the muddy Rynek to the drier

Poland's national poet, Mickiewicz

this huge square was laid out, it was the largest in Europe at roughly 40,000sq m (430,000sq ft).

Many Polish cities have allowed their medieval town squares to become museum-pieces while moving commerce elsewhere. Krakow's main square is still the heart of the modern city, as it was in the 14th century. Cafés and shops crowd its edges while a flower market and beer gardens fill the centre. Businessmen rub elbows with students, and lawyers make way for flocks of nuns on Rynek Główny's busy flagstones.

Each side of the Rynek repeats a pattern of three, evenly-spaced streets at right angles to the square, except for the southern corner where the much porch. To get to the storage cellars, deliverymen took a different set of stairs half a storey down. After one fire too many spread around the Rynek, wooden roofs over porches were banned by the Town Council in 1544, incidentally speeding the spread of Renaissance architecture in Krakow. Each successive paving project brought the level of the Rynek up a few centimetres until the porches became the street level.

Pomnik Mickiewicza (Monument to Mickiewicz)

The monument to the poet Adam Mickiewicz is familiarly known as 'Adaś' to the inhabitants of Krakow. It is a popular place for people to meet, before heading off to the bars and cafés of Old Town.

Mickiewicz, who was born in Belarus, spent his childhood in Lithuania and much of his adult years in Russia and France. His poem *Pan Tadeusz* is considered to be the Polish national epic and begins with the words 'O Lithuania, my homeland!' He died in Istanbul in 1855. Mickiewicz never visited Krakow while alive, but his body was re-interred under Wawel Cathedral in 1890.

The monument was unveiled in 1898, on the 100th anniversary of Mickiewicz's

The spirit of capitalism lives on in the Sukiennice

Obwazanki (Krakow pretzels) on sale on ul. Grodzka

birth. The figure on the tall central plinth represents the poet, and the four figures around the base are The Fatherland, Poetry, Valour and Science. In 1940, the Nazis broke the monument down and sold it for scrap. Miraculously, most of it was found in Hamburg after the war. Missing parts were recreated from the original designs and the monument was reconstructed in time for the 100th anniversary of Mickiewicz's death.

Sukiennice (The Cloth Hall)

About 1344, work began on a large Gothic brick Cloth Hall to replace the stalls in the centre of the square. Completed in 1392, it quickly became the most important commercial building in town.

Its appearance now is largely thanks to 16th-century rebuilding, which gave it those fine Renaissance gables – copied in many other buildings in Krakow. Many of the masks on the gables are from this period, though some are from the late 19th-century reconstruction, as are the long, colonnaded arcades along the sides. The ground floor is still home to commerce, mostly souvenir shops and cafés. Upstairs is now a gallery of the National Museum, housing turn-of-the-century art. *Tel: (012) 422 11 66. Open: Tue, Wed, Fri–Sun 10am–3pm; Thur 10am–5.30pm. Free admission Sun.*

Wieża Ratuszowa (The Town Hall Tower)

Krakow's Town Hall was built about 1300 as a low, square building with a single taller tower. In addition to chambers for the Town Council, it contained a court of justice, a jail, torture chambers and storage for merchants' goods. The Town Hall itself was demolished in 1817–20, leaving only its tower and cellars.

The upper storeys of the tower, now part of the Historical Museum, are entered from the stairway flanked with two stone lions. Legend claims that if a virtuous maiden sits on their backs, the lions will roar. Few Cracovian girls seem to put their virtue to the test these days. The interiors of the tower retain many Gothic features and the view from the top is fantastic. (*Opening hours change frequently.*)

The cellars (the ground floor when the Town Hall was first built) are entered from the opposite side of the building. They house a café and an underground stage. *Tel: (012) 422 99 22. Open: 10am–4 30pm. Admission charge.*

Plac Mariacki was once Krakow's main graveyard

In the national epic *Pan Tadeusz*, Adam Mickiewicz wrote: 'Such coffee as in Poland, there is in no other country ... it has the blackness of coal, the glow of amber, the aroma of mocha and the liquid thickness of honey'.

The first coffee house opened in Krakow in 1775 on the ground floor of Rynek Główny 31, now one of the very few buildings on the square that does not house a café. By the end of the 18th century, the coffee business was booming and a new Krakow tradition was born.

As the food critic Robert Makłowicz wrote, 'the need to be in cafés is for Cracovians something much more than merely consuming a cup of hot drink. It is a manifestation of a way of life, determinedly unhurried, still undefeated by the galloping destriers of business ...

they cannot refuse themselves dropping in for a cup of coffee in order to hear the latest gossip, to browse the newspapers on their special wooden racks or to indulge in their daily dose of title-mongering (Greetings, Mr. Editor! I kneel before you, my Dear Doctor! I bow to you, Lord Baron! I kiss thy hand, Honourable Barrister!). This typical Central European ritual has endured, unbroken by both benighted Bolshevism and Anglo-Saxon novelty. And thus it is that true Cracovians feel quite at home in Budapest, Vienna or Prague where similar tradition holds sway.'

The far-flung Habsburg Empire, with its capital in Vienna and territory that stretched from northern Italy to western Ukraine, was the perfect vehicle to spread the gospel of caffeine. Austrian,

proprietor, Jan Michalik accepted paintings and other works of art in payment. Much of his massive collection is still visible in the now subdued café on ul. Floriańska.

The mighty throng of Krakow's student population eagerly indulges in double espressos at trendy coffee bars like Tribeca or old standards like Vis-à-Vis to fuel up for late-night philosophical discussion or pre-exam study.

Discerning connoisseurs may pick the bean of their choice, be it Kenyan Mocha or Colombian Maragogipe at emporia like Pozegnanie z Afryka.

Even in the communist 1980s, there were 78 cafés doing business in Krakow, every one of them crowded with students, dissidents, artists and philosophers. Capitalism has allowed Cracovians to indulge themselves even further. Current estimates put the number of cafés at over 300 in the vicinity of Old Town and new ones are constantly opening.

Tadeusz Boy-Żeleński, a poet and doctor who outlived the golden years of *The Green Balloon* only to be killed by the Nazis, asked:

'And do you know those cafés
(in the whole world there are no others
* like these)*
where the whole day long, wastefully,
* wordily*
the miraculous bohemians mark time?'

There are plenty of coffee houses where you can sample a cup of the local brew

Swiss and Italian immigrants arrived to open chic, cosmopolitan coffee houses in Old Town, including the still-operating Redolfi (founded 1823) on Rynek Główny. Even Krakow's current Town Hall, the Pałac Wielopolskich, was the famous Austrian Winter's Cafeehaus until 1893.

The artistic demimonde that congregated in the strange chambers of Jama Michalika (Michalik's Den, founded 1895) staged a wild cabaret called *The Green Balloon*, full of song, poetry and puppet shows, which shocked the Victorian bourgeoisie of Krakow with their disrespectful caricatures. The king of the revels was Stanisław Przybyszewski whose bohemian lifestyle far outshone his artistic output. When the artists' money ran out, the

Cemeteries

Neath this deathly slab of stone that covers,
Born of Lubowiecki, Bursik's wife rests,
First amongst the citizens, at nineteen,
Consigned to this place by God's own order

reads the tombstone of a young bride, Apolonia Bursik *née* Lubowiecka, in Rakowicki cemetery. Poles take the adornment and maintenance of their loved ones' graves very seriously. Some of them spend more on dead relatives than on living ones – and it shows.

Cmentarz Podgórski

Two small cemeteries separated by a highway, in the hills across the river from Old Town (*see p108*).

Cmentarz Rakowicki

In 1795, Krakow was annexed to the Habsburg Empire, bringing its graveyards under Emperor Joseph II's recently-reformed burial laws. All urban cemeteries were to be closed at once, and the graves moved to new cemeteries beyond the edges of the city. For Cracovians, who had for centuries buried their dead in small cemeteries next to every church, this posed no small problem.

Cemeteries were set up outside Krakow, in Kleparz and Garbary, for the displaced dead but they filled up quickly. In 1800,

the city bought land in the nearby hamlet of Rakowice and began to lay out rows of plots. In 1803, Apolonia Bursik was the first citizen to be buried there. By 1836, with the reburial of bodies from churchyards and the newly dead of the city's growing population, the city had to buy more land, doubling the size of the graveyard.

Many slabs in Cmentarz Rakowicki support sculptures by the best artists of their time, like Xawery Dunikowski, Tadeusz Stryjeński and Teodor Talowski. A walk through Rakowicki is like an outdoor sculpture museum.

Cmentarz Remuh

The oldest Jewish cemetery still existing in Krakow (*see p101*).

ALL SAINTS' DAY

Hundreds of thousands of candles light up cemeteries across Poland on 1 November. After Christmas Eve, All Saints' Day is the most important family holiday on the Polish calendar. Most Poles will spend a few hours sprucing up their loved ones' graves before the big day and then, with the entire family, will lay flowers and candles on each slab. Families that have moved away from their ancestral lands will travel across Poland for the occasion. It may be the only time each year that far-flung families meet. Once prayers have been said and distant cousins greeted, a stroll through the fairyland of candles and flowers is in order.

Cmentarz Salwator

A small cemetery in the shadow of Kopiec Kościuszki (*see p116*).

Cmentarz Żydowski 'Nowy'

A large and still-functioning Jewish cemetery near Kazimierz (*see p99*).

Wawel and Skałka Necropolises

Krakow also has two burial crypts of special importance.

The Krypta Zasłużonych (the Crypt of the Worthy), under the Kościół św. Michała 'Na Skałce' in Kazimierz (*see p100*), contains the tombs of great writers and artists, in particular those of importance to the Polish sense of national identity.

The second crypt is the Groby Królewskie (the Royal Tombs) under the Cathedral on Wawel Hill (*see p83*). Not everyone buried there is royalty, however. Two poets (Mickiewicz and Słowacki), a military dictator (Pilsudski) and the head of the Polish government-in-exile during the Second World War (Sikorski) have been deemed worthy of resting among the dust of kings.

The final resting place of Cracovians great and small

The tree of life holds up Kościół św. Krzyża

Churches

The anonymous author of the first tourist guide to Krakow (in 1647) began with the words 'Krakow is a second Rome, for no day or hour passes without the sinner having some indulgence available here by visiting some church of holy place and saying prayers'.

Krakow's ostentatious devotion to the Roman Catholic Church can be surprising even to visitors from other Catholic countries. There are 87 churches and 56 monasteries in Krakow. Priests, monks and nuns are a common sight on the streets and devotional portraits of the Virgin Mary and the late Pope John Paul II are often placed in windows. The following are just the most famous churches.

Baroque crowns on Romanesque towers at Kościół św. Andrzeja

Katedra św. Stanisława (St Stanislaus' Cathedral)

(*see p80*)

Kościół św. Andrzeja (St Andrew's Church)

Begun about 1079, the church gained its massive shield-like wall facing the street and the two defensive towers in the 13th century. Those townspeople who did not gain a place up on Wawel were able to weather the bloody Tartar raid in 1241 by huddling inside this church's stout walls.

In contrast to the austere Romanesque exterior, the inside of the church was transformed into a whirlwind of overblown Baroque about 1700 by Baldassare Fontana. The pulpit, in the shape of a sailing ship, glides under the ornate organ.

Next door is a cloister of Poor Clares, founded in 1325. Legend claims that the nunnery and the church are kept clean by the ghost of a nun still trying to absolve the sins of the wicked life she led before joining the Order. In spite of the heavy remodelling and the equally heavy-handed 20th-century efforts to restore the original shape, Kościół św. Andrzeja remains the best example of a Romanesque building in Krakow.
ul. Grodzka 56.

Kościół św. Anny (St Ann's Church)
(see p69)

Kościół św. Benedykta (St Benedict's Church)
(see p110)

Kościół Bożego Ciała (Corpus Christi Church)
(see p99)

Kościół św. Floriana (St Florian's Church)

The original church from 1184 was founded by King Kazimierz II the Just to house the relics of St Florian, patron saint of fire brigades. Despite this, it burnt down in 1306 and was rebuilt several times. The bulk of the church is from the second half of the 17th century with major remodelling in the 18th and 19th centuries.

Krakow's pious 15th-century chronicles claim that when Pope Lucius III looked over his collection of saint's relics at Rome to pick a suitable patron for Krakow, St Florian's dead hand rose from his grave holding a card that read 'I want to go to Krakow'.

The Cracovian delegation managed to get the relics by wagon to the place that would later be Kleparz, about a kilometre (just over half a mile) north of the walls of Okół. At that point, the horses refused to go any further and the saint spoke from his tomb, asking for his church to be built on that spot. One of St Florian's arms is still encased in a silver reliquary in his church, but his head and other parts are now up in the Wawel Cathedral.
Corner of Plac Matejki and ul. Warszawska.

The voice of God moving over the waters at Kościół Franciszkanów

Kościół Franciszkanów (the Franciscan Church)

One of Krakow's oldest churches is also one of the most startling discoveries for a visitor. The original church was started in 1255 just across the moat from the north gate of the old walls of Okół but, by the time it was finished, Krakow had grown and the church was well within the new walls.

The 1436 rebuilding gave the Franciscan Church something like its current Gothic appearance but this was hidden under a crust of Baroque decoration in the 17th century. A fire in 1850 gave the opportunity to return the exterior to a semblance of its 15th-century self.

The interior, however, was turned over to a much bolder experiment. Rather than try to turn back the clock, the visionary Stanisław Wyspiański borrowed inspiration from the Gothic frescoes in Kościół Mariacki (which he had helped to restore) and merged it with a riotous explosion of Art Nouveau shapes and colours. The result is perhaps the single most moving work of turn-of-the-century Polish art.

Wyspiański also designed the dazzling stained glass. St Francis, the Blessed Salomea and the Elements stand behind the altar. The window that leaves the deepest impression, however, is 'God the Father Creating the World' over the west entrance.

Among the Baroque altars along the sides of the nave is a painting (1970) of St Maksymilian Kolbe, a Polish priest whose death in the Auschwitz concentration camp won him recognition as a martyr.

Jogaila, the pagan Grand Duke of Lithuania (c.1351–1434) was baptised here in 1386 to become Władysław Jagiełło, the Christian King of Poland. *ul. Franciszkańska.*

Kościół Jezuitów (the Jesuit Church)

Dedicated to the Most Sacred Heart of Jesus, the Jesuit Church is a highly eclectic cocktail of early Modernism with parts of Historicism that range from neo-Romanesque to neo-Baroque. Perhaps because it is so hard to classify, this unique building is often overlooked by guidebooks. Begun in 1909 on a plan by Mączyński, the interior harnessed the talents of many of the best Krakow artists of the early 20th century, especially Xavier Dunikowski's majestic sculptures over the entrances. The frescoes reach even further back in time to draw inspiration from early Roman Christianity and Byzantium. The overall effect is timeless – neither old nor new, neither traditional nor revolutionary. *ul. Kopernika 26.*

Kościół Karmelitów Na Piasku – Nawiedzenia Najświętszej Panny (the Carmelite Church on the Sands – the Visitation of the Most Holy Lady)

According to legend, in 1087, Prince Władysław Herman (1043–1102) suffered from a case of scurvy so awful that worms crawled in the rotting flesh of his face. Although the royal doctors were unable to cure the disease, the Virgin Mary appeared to the prince and told him to travel west out of the city to a place where wild violets bloomed. The sand there would cure his disease and the prince should found a church on the spot in thanksgiving.

During 1395–9, Jadwiga and Jagiełło began work on a Gothic church here.

The church houses a miraculous icon of the Virgin Mary from the turn of the 16th century. A monk assigned to decorating the side chapel (to the right as you enter the church) sketched out the design for a fresco of the Virgin Mary holding the baby Jesus but left the colouring for the next day. When he returned to his sketch, he found some angelic hand had miraculously completed it. During the Swedish invasion of Poland (1656) the church was pulled down by the Protestant troops, but the fresco of the Virgin Mary somehow remained intact.

The church, rebuilt in 17th-century style, borrows much of the façade from Kościół św. Piotra i Pawła (*ul. Grodzka, see p46*) but on a much more humble scale. In 1683, Jan III Sobieski prayed here before setting out to relieve the

siege of Vienna, an event commemorated on a plaque just above Jadwiga's footprint. The rainbow-hued Calvary on the corner is from the 18th century.
ul. Karmelicka 19 (corner of ul. Garbarska).

Kościół św. Katarzyny (St Catherine's Church)
(*see p99*)

Kościół N.M.P. Królowej Polski 'Arka' (B.V.M. Queen of Poland Church 'the Ark')
(*see p126*)

Kościół św. Krzyża (Holy Cross Church)
A wooden church was erected on this spot at the turn of the 13th century. In 1244, the church was handed over to the neighbouring Hospital of the Holy Spirit, whose symbol was the double cross, which appears in several places around the church. The current limestone and brick structure was built at some time in the 14th century. In 1892, the large complex of buildings associated with the Hospital was levelled to make way for the Teatr Słowacki, in spite of loud protests from Krakow's historians and artists. The only buildings that survive are the Scholars Hospital (now Dom Pod Krzyżem at ul. Szpitalna 21), the church itself and a Gothic monastic building at ul. św. Krzyża 23, now the vicarage of the church.
Pl. św. Ducha (just off ul. Szpitalna).

Kościół św. Małgorzaty (St Margaret's Church)
(*see p117*)

Kościół Mariacki (St Mary's Church)
The silhouette of Kościół Mariacki dominates Rynek Główny and remains a recognisable landmark on the horizon even out in the hills around the city. As you face the church, the left-hand tower is topped with a thinner, eight-sided upper storey (1400–08) and a late-Gothic peak (1478). The shorter, right-hand tower's crown was finished much later, in 1548 (*see* The Two Towers *pp50–51*).

The church's mix of red brick and pale limestone is typical of Gothic structures in Krakow. The three large churches that were built (Bożego Ciała and św. Katarzyna) or extensively renovated (Kościół Mariacki) in the

St Mary's Church

reign of King Kazimierz the Great all share this style, but to very different effects.

Parallel to the Cathedral's role on Wawel as the church of the royal court, Kościół Mariacki was the primary church of the burghers. The small square around the church was their graveyard (*see pp30–31*) and against the outside walls still stand many funerary chapels and plaques to rich merchant families. This was also a place of public justice: citizens who broke the law could find

The Assumption of the Virgin Mary

themselves in the iron shackles by the south door (halfway between the main entrance and the one marked 'for tourists').

The full dedication of the church is the Basilica of the Assumption of the Blessed Virgin Mary, but it is always known to Cracovians as Kościół Mariacki (the Marian Church). There are several smaller shrines to Mary in her various aspects inside the church. The most important is a copy of the Black Madonna – Matka Boska Częstochowska (the original is in Częstochowa) – ornamented with a papal crown (1968) bestowed by Cardinal Stefan Wyszyński (1901–81).

The crowning glory of Kościół Mariacki is the altar screen carved by the Nuremburg sculptor known as Wit Stwosz in Poland and as Veit Stoss in the German lands. Stwosz (1438–1533) kept a workshop in Krakow in the years 1477–92, where he and his disciples produced many of the finest examples of late Gothic sculpture anywhere in Europe.

The altarpiece is essentially a huge cabinet in three pieces, which can be opened or closed. The frame is oak, but the sculptures are plane wood, a tree closely associated with the Virgin Mary. When open, the wings reveal six joys in the life of Mary. When closed, they display 12 sorrows. The central scene is the Assumption. Mary is shown fainting away into the arms of John while, above their heads, her figure is repeated as she is taken up into Heaven. Finally, above the frame of the screen, she is seen once again, being crowned in Heaven, flanked by Saints Adalbert and Stanisław.

This magnificent work of art contains about 200 human figures, each in a dynamic, almost voluptuous, pose with eyes rolling and hands gesturing as swirls of golden fabrics billow in unseen winds. When Pablo Picasso stood before Stwosz's masterpiece in 1948, he is reported to have exclaimed 'but this is the eighth wonder of the world!' *Open: Mon–Sat 11.30am–6pm, Sun 2–6pm. Admission charge.*

Kościół św. Michała i klasztor Paulinów (St Michael's Church and the Pauline Fathers' Monastery)
(*see p100*)

Kościół św. Mikołaja (St Nicholas' Church)
The first church dedicated to St Nicholas was an early 12th-century Romanesque edifice on the road east to Kiev. It is now a very subdued example of late 17th-century Baroque, but bits and pieces of many styles, especially Gothic polychrome and stones from the Romanesque walls, show through in various places.

In front of the church is a sandstone 'lantern of the dead' which in the 14th century stood in front of the leprosarium church of St Valentine's in Kleparz. It was moved here in 1871 after its home church was destroyed and is the only remaining example in Krakow of a once-common churchyard feature. *ul. Kopernika.*

Kościół i klasztor Norbertanek (The Premonstratensian Nuns' Church and Cloister)
(*see p118*)

Kościół Pijarów (the Piarist Church)
One of the youngest churches in Old Town, it was designed by Rome-educated Kacper Bażanka (1680–1726) who was not only an architect but also Krakow's mayor. Work began in 1714. The result is a remarkably poised and graceful late Baroque church with a slightly later (1759–61) Rococo façade.

To each side of the central shrine stand two monastic wings, one of which has been redecorated in a neo-Gothic style and now houses part of the Czartoryski Museum.

The intellectual discipline of the church's rhythm and balance continues into the interior decorations. Much of the work shows influences from Moravia, thanks to the large number of artisans imported from Brno to complete the dancing display of arches and Corinthian columns.
Corner of ul. św Jana and ul. Pijarskiej.

St Nicholas' Church

Kościół św. Piotra i Pawła
(Sts Peter and Paul's Church)

Begun in 1597, the first fully Baroque church in Krakow, Kościół św. Piotra i Pawła is an intentional copy of the Jesuit Church 'Il Gesú' in Rome. Zygmunt III financed its construction, on the recommendation of the influential Jesuit preacher Piotr Skarga (1563–1612), whose body lies below the church and whose monument stands opposite the entrance on a pillar. Although Skarga was never officially made a saint, Cracovians often leave prayers and requests on little slips of paper at his tomb.

The Italian Jesuit architects evidently tried to harmonise their design with the cityscape of Krakow. The dizzying cupola above the nave follows the Roman model inside but clearly borrows much of its exterior from the Renaissance Zygmunt Chapel attached to the Wawel Cathedral. The monumental line of 12 apostles along the fence dividing the church from ul. Grodzka was designed by Bażanka during 1715–22.

The vast interior makes use of a highly developed knowledge of acoustics, so that the Jesuits' Counter-Reformation sermons could be heard throughout the church. The tall dome offers the highest straight drop from any ceiling in Krakow, hence the Foucault's Pendulum which demonstrates that the earth does turn on its axis.

When the Jesuits were temporarily dissolved in 1773, their church and the college next to it were turned over to other uses. The college now belongs to its old rival, the Jagiellonian University. The church was for a few years (1809–15) assigned to the Eastern Orthodox congregation of Krakow but is now used by a Catholic parish.
ul. Grodzka.

The dome of Kościół św. Piotra i Pawła

Kościół Najświętszego Salwatora
(Church of the Most Holy Saviour)

(*see p118*)

Kościół św. Wojciecha (St Adalbert's Church)

This tiny, almost cubical, church stands in one corner of Rynek Główny, completely at odds with the regular gridiron pattern of streets around it. Its strange orientation lines up with that of Kościół Mariacki and ul. Grodzka, a sure sign that it is older than the town plan of 1257. The first church on the site seems to have been built on top of a burial mound, beside the track leading north out of Okół. The current Romanesque church was built on the same foundations at some time in the 12th century. It was updated to the Baroque style, visible at the upper layers of the building, in the 17th and 18th centuries. Later conservators cut away portions of these additions to reveal the original building. The Romanesque portal, now nearly 2m (6ft) below the surface of Rynek Główny, shows the level of the square in the 13th century.

Tribute to a local hero

BIOGRAPHY, POPE JOHN PAUL II

'Stay with us!' the Cracovian crowds chanted at each of Pope John Paul II's visits to his old flock. Karol Wojtyła, the Pope, was archbishop of Krakow from 1963 to 1978. He oversaw some of this deeply Roman Catholic city's greatest triumphs against communism, including building the church popularly known as 'the Ark' in the socialist model city of Nowa Huta.

Born in the town of Wadowice, 40km (25 miles) to the southwest, Karol Wojtyła came to Krakow as a Polish Literature student of the Jagiellonian University, where he made an early impression as a poet and actor. When the Second World War broke out, the university was closed by the Nazis. Wojtyła continued his studies at night in the 'underground' university, where his focus changed to theology. During the day, he was a forced labourer in a German-run stone quarry.

Wojtyła became a priest in 1946 and served in various roles in Krakow parishes. In 1978, he was chosen as the first non-Italian Pope since the Avignon Schism. His election had special meaning to the people of communist Poland and inspired mass demonstrations like the White March after the 1981 assassination attempt in which 900,000 Cracovians marched peacefully through the streets, dressed in white. His moral support for the Solidarity movement has often been credited with bringing down communism. John Paul II died 2 April 2005, greatly mourned by the Polish people.

Walk: Rynek Główny, the main market square

Nearly every Polish schoolchild makes a pilgrimage to Krakow and dutifully visits the famous sights. 'As round as the Krakow Rynek …' (that is, not round at all) is a phrase that you are more likely to hear from a native of Warsaw than of Krakow.

Allow 1 hour.

Begin at the busy northeast corner of Rynek Główny where ul. Floriańska enters the square.

1 Around Kościół Mariacki

In front of you are the twin spires of Kościół Mariacki (the Marian Church, *see pp43–4*). Follow the side of the church away from the main square and pass the funerary chapels at the back of the church. Pass into Mały Rynek (*see p30*), once Krakow's vegetable market. Turn right alongside the building and right again through the tunnel-like passage back into Plac Mariacki (*see pp30–31*).

Head across the square back towards the bustle of Rynek Główny.

Notice the shackles by the south door, for punishing sinners.

2 Mickiewicz

Entering Rynek Główny, you face the long building of the Sukiennice (Cloth Hall, *see pp34–5*). The Town Hall Tower rises behind it. To the left of the Sukiennice stands the monument to Adam Mickiewicz (*see p33*) where would-be teenage Romeos nervously wait *pod Adasiem* (under Adam) for their dates.

Turn left and follow the edge of the square.

3 św. Wojciecha and Pod Jaszczurami

At No. 8 on the square you come to a *kamienica* known as Pod Jaszczurami (Under the Lizards) after the entwined reptiles over the door. Pop in to see the ribbed Gothic ceilings. Across from Pod Jaszczurami is the small church of św. Wojciecha (St Adalbert's).

Continue to the mouth of ul. Grodzka.

4 Grodzka and Hetmańska

Continuing to follow the square clockwise, you come to the Wierzynek Restaurant (the legendary site of Wierzynek's famous banquet, *see p64*) and the huge Kamienica Hetmańska (Commander's Townhouse, *see pp64–5*). Stop in the Hetmańska bookshop (at No. 17) to peek at the Gothic rondels in the ceiling. Further along is the Kamienica Pod Obrazem No. 18 (House Under the Picture) with its huge icon of the Virgin Mary (painted in 1718) dominating the façade.

Continue clockwise to the next corner and turn right.

5 Pod Kruki, Pałac Pod Baranami, Wieża Ratuszowa

At No. 25, Kamienica Pod Kruki (House Under the Sign of the Ravens) is an international cultural centre. The Pałac Pod Baranami (Palace Under the Sign of the Rams, *see p75*), with its famous cabaret in the cellars, is opposite. The lonely tower in the corner of the square is the only surviving fragment of Krakow's once spacious Town Hall (*see p35*).
Continue following the square clockwise.

6 Pałac Krzysztofory and ul. Szczepańska

Following the line of buildings, you pass a small monument to Piotr Skrzynecki (1930–97). Cross the mouth of ul. Szewska (Tailor's Street) and continue to the corner of the square, where the Pałac Krzysztofory houses the main branch of the Historical Museum of Krakow (*see p93*). Just across the street, Dom Pod Gruszką (House Under the Sign of the Pear, *ul. Szczepańska 1*) is a journalist's club with a restaurant and fantastic Baroque ceilings.

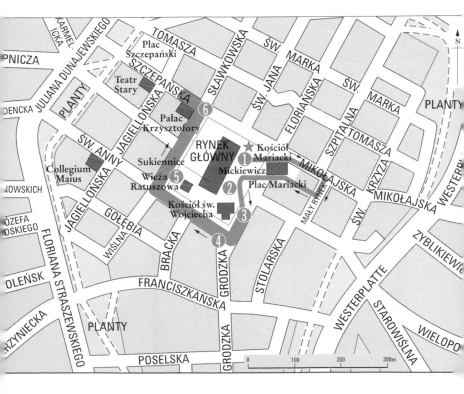

Cracovians love their legends with a fierce passion. Nearly every building in town boasts a ghost, demon, monster, magician or tragic lover. Some buildings have two or three.

The Bugler at the Gates of Dawn

Every hour, on the hour, a bugler high up in the taller of the Mariacki church towers opens a little window and plays a bugle call. He then repeats the awkward melody from three more windows.

Tourists are piously told how in 1241 the watchman in the Mariacki church tower saw the Tartars preparing to invade the city. He blew his trumpet to warn the townspeople but a sharp-eyed Tartar bowman cut short the warning with a well-placed arrow that pierced the watchman's throat. The townspeople, however, had been alerted. Afterwards, in memory of the brave trumpeter, the *hejnał* was always played to the note on which the arrow struck, and no further.

The most likely explanation for the lost origin of the *hejnał* is that it arrived with King Louis the Hungarian or his daughter Queen Jadwiga at the end of the 14th century. *Hejnał* means 'dawn'

in Hungarian and the trumpet call may have been the signal to open the city gates in the morning. At the four main city gates a trumpeter could complete the melody to indicate that the gate was open. The *hejnał* was repeated in the evening, probably when the gates were closed. It was not until the 17th century that the *hejnał* began to be played every hour.

The Two Towers

The two towers of the Mariacki church are of very different heights: 81m and 69m (266ft, 226ft). Legend claims that two brothers were employed to oversee the building work. The older brother was confident and began to build quickly. The younger brother was more cautious and carefully prepared the foundations. As the elder brother built higher quickly, he was forced to make each storey slightly shorter and narrower than the one before to keep the tower stable. The younger brother, however, knew his well-prepared base was solid and continued to build each storey broad and tall. The elder brother realised that his younger brother's creation would outdo his own in the end. In a fit of jealousy, he stabbed his sibling with an iron knife and then, overcome with remorse, confessed and threw himself off his own tower. According to legend, the townspeople hung the murder weapon from a chain near the entrance to the Sukiennice in memory of the brothers.

In reality, the two towers were built to more-or-less the same height; then, 70 years later, additional storeys were added to one of them. An iron knife really does hang from a chain in the Sukiennice. It symbolised the swift and sharp justice of medieval law to all the merchants who passed under it.

The Prince's Enchanted Knights

At the end of the 13th century, several princes were attempting to consolidate their claims to be King of Poland. Prince Henryk IV the Honest (c. 1257–90) gained control of Wrocław and Krakow and felt that he could be king if he had the support of the pope. Unfortunately, the prince had no money to travel to Rome. A witch offered Henryk a loan if he left his retinue of knights behind as collateral. He agreed and the witch transformed his friends into pigeons. They flew up to the walls of the Mariacki church and gold rained down on the square below. Henryk gathered up the money and set off for Rome. Unfortunately, he gambled and drank the money away before he got to Italy and had to return to Krakow without crown or knights. In 1290, he was poisoned by a rival.

The Devil in the Beer Cellar

An old tale tells how a servant girl was sent to Rynek Główny to buy chickens for a feast, but one escaped and ran into the cellars of the haunted Krzysztofory Palace. The poor girl had no choice but to follow the bird. She got lost in the huge labyrinth that runs under the square and, after blundering around in the dark for hours, came face to face with a devil sitting on a huge pile of gold. He offered to let her take as much gold as she could carry, on one condition. When leaving the cellars, she must not look back. Like Orpheus before her, she forgot and looked back just as she was stepping up to the ground floor. The door slammed shut and chopped off the heel of her foot. According to some versions of the story, her gold turned to dross. Others say she kept the gold, won a good husband in spite of her maimed foot and founded a chapel in Kościół Mariacki.

This chapel in Kościół Mariacki is Kaplica św. Antoniego (Chapel of St Anthony), where condemned prisoners prayed before their execution.

Opposite: No Tartars in sight
Above: The uneven towers of Kościół Mariacki

Walk: The 'Royal Way' (Floriańska Gate to Wawel)

Even after the royal court moved to Warsaw in 1609, coronations were still held in Krakow until 1734. Arriving from Warsaw, the Kościół św. Floriana in Kleparz was the last stop for rest and prayer before the future king entered the city. He would then pass down ul. Floriańska through ul. Grodzka to Wawel Cathedral.

Allow 1 hour.

Begin at the red-brick barbican, just outside Floriańska gate.

1 Barbakan

The Grunwald Monument (a 1976 copy), commemorating the battle of Grunwald (1410) can be seen if you look north while standing by the outer fortifications. Beyond, you can see the towers of Kościół św. Floriana.

Pass through the Floriańska Gate and into the Old Town.

The Sukiennice

2 Floriańska

At No. 45 is Jama Michalika (Michalik's Den) a museum that serves coffee. At No. 13 the antique gallery DESA has 16th-century frescoes and the private Space Gallery has slightly newer ones from the 17th century.

Continue out into the main square.

3 Rynek Główny

At this point you could split off to loop around the Rynek Główny walk (*see p48*) or continue straight along the line of buildings passing Kościół Mariacki on your left. On your right is the Sukiennice.

Pass through the Rynek and on to ul. Grodzka.

4 Grodzka and Plac Wszystkich Świętych

Another important shopping street, ul. Grodzka leads from the 13th-century town centre to the oldest part of Old Town. Plac Wszystkich Świętych was once the site of Kościół Wszystkich

Świętych (All Saints' Church). Both this church and the still-standing Franciscan Church (*see pp41–2*) were just outside the walls of pre-1257 Krakow. The building to the right is the Pałac Wielopolskich (*see p76*), now the Town Hall. A monument to Józef Dietl (1804–78), Rector of the Jagiellonian University and President of the City of Krakow, stands over the square. *Continue straight along ul. Grodzka crossing ul. Poselska and ul. Senacka.*

5 Plac św. Marii Magdaleny

To your right is the ancient seat of the Law Department of the Jagiellonian University (*see p68*), now the Art History Department and home to a small butterfly museum. The 11th-century church of St Andrew's (*see p40*) was the town's religious centre in times of peace and its fortress in times of danger. Next to this the Baroque Kościół św. Piotra i Pawła (*see p46*) was built half a millennium later. The square, Plac św. Marii Magdaleny (Mary Magdalene's Square, *see p31*), was named after a church which was pulled down in 1811. At the back of the square is a museum to Stanisław Wyspiański.
Continue straight along ul. Grodzka.

6 At the base of Wawel Hill

On the left you pass the 17th-century Lutheran church of St Martin's. At the end of ul. Grodzka, stands the tiny Gothic Kościół św. Idziego (St Giles' Church). A cross stands in front of the church in memory of the Polish officers shot by the Soviets in Katyn Forest.
You may continue by turning right at the church and taking the walk on p88: Wawel, the Polish Acropolis.

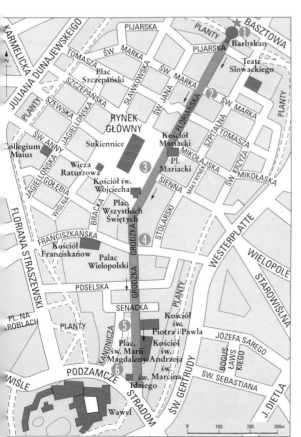

Like Rome, 'Krakow was not built in a day' as Cracovians like to say. A barbarian stronghold adopted Romanesque architecture and was slowly transformed into a European capital. Remains of earlier times are all around if you know where to look.

In the 10th century, the Slavs along the Wisła valley began to adopt the artistic styles of their western neighbours along with Christianity. Wood remained the norm in private homes and fortifications, but first churches and then the 'palatia' of the powerful nobility began to be built in stone.

The Piast kings borrowed Ottonian styles of early Romanesque. Their early attempts were smaller scale and less graceful than their Saxon models, and inferior in craftsmanship. Little of this primitive phase has survived. The base of the rotunda of Sts Felix and Adauctus was built into the foundations of the castle kitchens and was only rediscovered in 1917.

The age of confident Romanesque in Krakow begins with Kazimierz I the Restorer who brought his court to the city about 1038. He built a new stone palace and a basilica (of which only fragments remain) on Wawel.

On a smaller scale, you can still see much Romanesque work under the Baroque crust of Kościół św. Wojciecha (St Adalbert's Church). Built beside the road a few hundred metres north of the city moat, it now finds itself in the main square.

Although the Wawel Cathedral of Prince Władysław Herman has gone, the serene gloom of the crypt of St Leonard (1118) is still witness to the strength and durability of the Romanesque. It now houses the Royal Tombs.

New religious orders from the south, the Franciscans and Dominicans, in the 13th century brought more cosmopolitan touches to the heavy Germanic style. The Tartar invasion of 1241, however, left wooden buildings in flames and stone ones in rubble. When rebuilding began in earnest, architects were already under the influence of the Gothic.

Churches were also built down below in Okół and on the main routes out of the city.

Fragments of earlier masonry may be seen in several Krakow churches, but one whole Romanesque building survives: the limestone fortress–church of św. Andrzeja (St Andrew's). It was the parish church but also a refuge in times of war.

Opposite: Stained glass in Wawel Cathedral
Above: A Romanesque tower at Kościół św. Andrzeja that helped to fend off the Tartar invasion of 1241

Cycling is a great way to see Krakow's green spaces

Gardens and Parks

Like many medieval towns, Krakow was densely settled, leaving little space for greenery. Outside the walls were open swathes of pasture, one of which has survived as the Błonia park. As the old walls were pulled down, public parks and boulevards began to appear. The 'garden city' of English town planner Sir Ebenezer Howard (1850–1928) made an impression on Krakow architects of the early 20th century, who integrated parks and greenery into the layout of suburbs like Salwator. Today 112 parks, public gardens and green boulevards pump much-needed oxygen into the city.

Błonia (Meadows)

That this huge triangle of green lawn could survive in the heart of Krakow is a miracle of stubborn tradition and enlightened planning. The Norbertine Convent traded it in 1366 for a *kamienica* in Krakow, and Błonia (Meadows) became common pasture for the people of Zwierzyniec and Krakow. The pasture was whittled away by encroaching settlements until its boundaries were fixed in 1908. Many attempts since to exploit this valuable property have failed, as Cracovians proudly cling to their right to graze cattle and sheep there.

The Błonia field has been the site of many important events, including the first aeroplane flight from Krakow in 1910 and Pope John Paul II's huge masses for millions of Poles. On warm Sunday mornings you can even find expatriates and their friends playing baseball or cricket here.
Between Al. Focha and Al. 3-go Maja.

Ogród Botaniczny (Botanical Gardens)

Established in 1783 by the rector of the university, the Botanical Gardens occupy the grounds of a palace in Wesoła. The university acquired it when the Jesuits were outlawed in 1773. Krakow's Botanical Gardens became among the largest in Europe in the 19th century, with formal French-style geometric gardens and naturalistic English-style parks. Greenhouses were erected for tropical plants.

Nazi officers looted the gardens for houseplants to decorate their homes and offices, while the rest was left to wither and die. The reconstructed gardens now cover 9.8 hectares (24 acres) with 6,000 varieties of plants. Among the spectacular sights are the greenhouse dedicated to palm trees and the 400-year-old 'Jagiellonian Oak'. The best time to visit is spring when the gardens burst into flower.
Entrance from ul. Kopernika.

Park Jordana (Jordan's Park)

A great educational reformer, Professor Henryk Jordan (*see* Children *p157*), inspired and partly funded this big park designed for children. He also brought football to Krakow for the first time in 1890.

Planty (Plantations)

This ring of greenery encircling Old Town is roughly 4km (2½ miles) around. It was planned by Feliks Radwański to fill the space left by demolition of the city defences in 1810–14. Work started on the gardens in 1820 and Cracovians called them *planty* (plantations).

The terrain was low and wet (because of the double moat), but soon dried out, so artificial pools and fountains were added to the original design. In 1874, the first sculpture, an obelisk near the railway station, was added. Since then, many statues have been erected in the gardens of important figures from Polish history and literature. In 1992, the old line of the walls was marked out and

Strolling in the Planty, the ring of greenery surrounding Old Town

plaques were set up at the site of each tower.

The Planty are a useful landmark for travellers unfamiliar with Krakow. The centre of Old Town always lies more-or-less at right angles to the concave edge of the gardens.

ŚWIATOWID

The mysterious four-faced pagan idol at the foot of Wawel Hill was erected in 1968 on the 800th anniversary of the fall of Arkona, the last great Slavic temple. Offerings of flowers, candles and food can often be found at its base.

The monument below Wawel is a faithful copy of the original idol, which now rests in the Archaeological Museum (*see pp92–3*). It was found in the River Zbrucz (now in Ukraine) in 1848. Although no-one knows what the people who carved it called their idol, it has become popularly known as Światowid after the four-headed idol of *Svantovitvs* at Arkona, destroyed by the Danish King Valdemar I in 1168.

The (10th-century?) limestone idol has four bas-relief faces, each divided into three horizontal layers. Many theorise that the bottom layer with a three-headed, kneeling figure represents the underworld. The middle layer, with four small human figures, is thought to be the world of mortal men. The upper layer may represent four gods – or four aspects of one god. One side shows a god holding a ring, another is holding a horn, on the third side it seems to be riding a horse and carrying a sword. The final side shows the god's empty hands folded against its chest.

Walk: Planty (old city walls)

In the summer, the green ring of the Planty gardens becomes Krakow's promenade. Young lovers hold hands in a lazy stroll. Parents chase after wandering children. Pensioners take their pets for a walk.

Allow 1 hour.

Begin on the east side, just south of the end of ul. Mikołajska, where it crosses the Planty gardens (a little towards ul. Sienna).

1 The Butchers' Gate

This walled-up gate was once the entrance to the Butchers' Quarter of Old Town Krakow. It is now part of the Dominican Convent known as Na Gródku (On the Fortress). The fortress is long gone, dismantled after the unsuccessful Revolt of Castellan Albert in 1311–12. Following the line of the walls anti-clockwise, walk northwards. The mouth of ul. Mikołajska once had outer fortifications, a smaller version of the barbican. Continuing further, you can see a low stone wall marking the old defences. There are plaques every 10m (30ft) or so to mark the site of an old tower. The first north of Mikołajska is the Capmakers' Tower. On your left, you come to the unique one-column Gothic church of the Holy Cross (*see p43*) and the bright yellow, neo-Baroque Teatr Słowackiego. To your right, is the monument to Florian Straszewski, one of the designers of the Planty gardens. It stands where an earth mound was raised in honour of the short-lived Free City of Krakow. The mound was destroyed by the Austro-Hungarian authorities when the Free City was re-annexed by the Empire.

Continue anti-clockwise.

2 The Barbican and Floriańska Gate

After crossing ul. Szpitalna, you come to the last free-standing section of Krakow's old walls. The first tower is the Haberdashers' Tower, followed by the Floriańska Gate (*see p28*). Pass between the Floriańska Gate and the Barbican to the Joiners' and Carpenters' towers. The rest of the towers have been torn down, but thanks to renovations in the 1990s you can still trace most of their course in the coloured paving. At the mouth of ul. Sławkowska there was another fortified gate. The monument (1886) of Queen Jadwiga and King Jagiełło holding a cross (they Christianised Lithuania) was originally planned to be for Princess Dąbrówka and Prince Mieszko (who Christianised Poland).

Continue anti-clockwise.

3 Pałac Sztuki

Between ul. Tomasza and ul. Szczepańska is the Art Nouveau Palace of Art (*see p96*). The monument to artist Artur Grottger (1837–67), opposite, was designed to be part of an aesthetic whole with the palace. Further along, you come to the lively outdoor café in front of the avant-garde Bunkier Sztuki (*see p92*). The mysterious knee-high brick walls in the middle of ul. Szewska are a very fragmentary reconstruction of the old gate.

Continue anti-clockwise, now going south.

4 Collegium Novum and the Archaeological Museum

Below the neo-Gothic red brick of Collegium Novum (*see p68*) is a monument to Copernicus, one of the most famous students of the Jagiellonian University. The only surviving relic of neo-Gothic ornamentation of Collegium Maius, it was moved here in the 1950s. The tree in front of the building is known as the Freedom Tree, planted on the first anniversary of Poland's 1919 independence. Continuing to where ul. Wiślna crosses the Planty, you can see the cupola of Krakow's Greek Catholic church. Further along, the gardens are cut by tram tracks that run next to the Franciscan Church and Monastery (*see pp41–2*). The old walls past ul. Poselska are those of the old town prison. The prison is now the Archaeological Museum (*see pp92–3*).

Continue along the Planty towards the Wawel Hill.

5 At the foot of Wawel

Passing the monument to Tadeusz Boy-Żeleński, a doctor, poet and translator who died in the Warsaw uprising, you come to the foot of Wawel Hill.

You might return via ul. Floriańska by turning left at Grodzka or you can continue by following the walk on p88: Wawel, the Polish Acropolis.

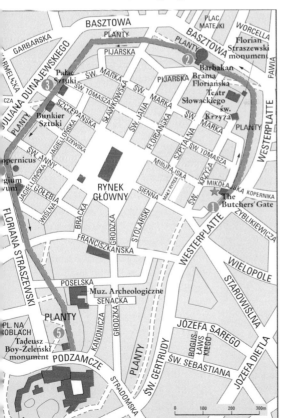

The purpose of the delicate, brightly-coloured architectural fantasies on sale in the souvenir shops may seem a bit of a mystery to visitors until they peer into the recesses of the central balcony to see the tiny figures of Joseph and Mary bent over a manger.

True Cracovian *szopki*, as they are called, must be hand-made in bright and shiny colours. They may be large or small but they must include recognisable elements borrowed from Krakow's architecture, fusing Gothic with Renaissance and Baroque in an anachronistic amalgam. They often include characters from local legends, such as Pan Twardowski or the Wawel Dragon, as well as politicians,

professors, artists and other recognisable Cracovian citizens. Plus they must include somewhere, among the many figures that crowd the scene, the Nativity of Jesus.

The origins of the Krakow *szopki* may be found with St Francis of Assisi in 13th-century Italy. He popularised Christmas cribs as a way to bring the Nativity story to the illiterate masses. The idea was brought to Krakow with the Franciscan order and flourished. The immobile figures of the first cribs became puppets and the story of the Nativity was acted out in *jasełki* (folk puppet shows).

Unemployed building workers made *jasełki* in order to eke out their income in winter. One way they lured their rivals' customers was by building bigger and fancier scenery. They began to glue bits of shiny paper from sweets on to their structures and include moving parts like spinning wheels. They also borrowed architectural elements from the city around them so that a manger in Bethlehem might sprout a gable from the Sukiennice and towers from Kościół Mariacki.

Up until the 19th century, *szopki* remained centred on the scene of the Nativity. At the end of the century, two brothers, Leon and Michał Ezenekier, bricklayers from Krowodrza, changed all that. They consigned the Nativity to immobile figures in an upper gallery, leaving their imaginations unfettered for the rest. As the Nativity shrank,

other portions grew larger and more complex, incorporating more and more architectural elements.

Puppeteers had discovered that their shows were the only form of theatre untouched by Austro-Hungarian censorship. Caricature puppets of local authorities could disappear instantly when a constable passed, and the improvised dialogue had no script for bureaucrats to check. With the Holy Family safely ensconced on their balcony, the puppet shows ranged far from the gospels.

In the 20th century, radio began to cut into the audience for live performance but the fantastic *szopki* had established themselves as an essential part of Krakow Christmas. Enterprising boys began to sell smaller versions of traditional *szopki* – with little statues in place of puppets – for families to set up at home.

Dr Jerzy Dobrzycki (1900–72), an art historian, initiated the first *szopki* contest in December 1937 to help preserve this unique local tradition. In the beginning, prizes were given informally by private citizens, and included bottles of wine and hams. When Dobrzycki became Director of the Historical Museum of Krakow after the Second World War, the contest became formally organised by the museum.

Although the number of participants has dropped, the contest is still held on the first Thursday of December. The *szopki* are first displayed around the base of the monument to Adam Mickiewicz until noon and are then paraded into the museum where they are judged. They remain on display in the smaller gallery to the right of the main entrance until February.

Szopki on display

Kamienice: Patrician and Burgher Houses

One of the most distinctive elements of Old Town Krakow is the preponderance of a single type of house, the *kamienica*. With roots in the 13th century, the standard Krakow *kamienica* remained a fundamental of urban planning up to the 19th century.

Bird's-eye view of ul. Floriańska

The evolution of the Krakow *kamienica* (townhouse) is paralleled elsewhere in Central Europe, but it remains a distinct local type, originating in the plots laid out by the 1257 town plan: eight parcels of roughly 42m × 21m (140ft × 70ft) in each block. Most owners split their parcels lengthwise into two narrow strips, each with a 10m (33ft) frontage.

The parcel was typically divided into three: a stone-and-brick front building, an open courtyard and a wooden back building. Courtyards were usually separated from buildings alongside by high walls, on which wooden galleries sometimes ran, connecting upper storeys of the front building with the back.

The front building usually had a large entrance hall at ground level, leading to the courtyard and flanked by a shop or other public space. Families lived in the upper storeys. There was storage space in the warm attic for dry goods like grain and in the cool cellars for foodstuffs like beer, giving them their Polish name, *piwnice*.

Krakow's *kamienice* lost their peaked Gothic gables when 16th-century fire regulations required walls between buildings. Renaissance gables, or attics, were straight across, not peaked, and were often decorated with fantastic masks, coats of arms or organic shapes.

Dom Pod Pająkiem (House Under the Sign of the Spider)

The innovative Galician artist Teodor Talowski (1857–1910) built this house for himself in 1889. The spider rests in her web at the top of the façade. Two smaller spiders lurk in the metalwork of the doors. The spider is associated with Pan Twardowski (*see p63*) as well as being a suitable metaphor for the architect's trade.

In this, as in his other buildings, Talowski mixed Historicism, Romanticism and the heady brew of Art Nouveau into an eclectic architecture of irregular but graceful buildings adorned with greenery, fanciful beasts and Latin mottoes. The House Under the Sign of the Spider shows particularly strong borrowings from Dutch mannerism. Talowski intentionally selected irregularly-shaped and over-baked bricks rejected by other builders to give his home even more character. *ul. Karmelicka 35 (corner of ul. Batorego). Trams: 4, 8, 13, 14, 24.*

Dom Pod Śpiewającą Żabą

Designed by Talowski, the large corner building known as Pod Śpiewającą Żabą (Under the Sign of the Singing Frog) was built during 1889–90. The name comes from the debonair frog silently crooning from the top of this building, playing his mandolin. He reminds us that this street was alive with the croaking of frogs when the house was built: the green strip down the centre of the street marks the old bed of the Rudawa river, covered over in 1910. Nearby are four more houses by Talowski, three of which bear mottoes: *Festina lente* (Hurry slowly) and *Ars longa, vita brevis* (Art lasts long but life is short) at No. 7, *Faber est suae quisque fortunae* (Each man is smith of his own fortune) at No. 9, and *Długo myśl, prędko czyń* (Think long, act quickly) at No. 15.

ul. Retoryka 1.
Trams: 15, 18; Bus: 124.

Under the sign of the spider

PAN TWARDOWSKI

According to Krakow legend, Pan Twardowski was a 16th-century minor nobleman and magician. He made a pact with the Devil, who granted his every wish in exchange for his soul, to be paid over when the nobleman made a trip to Rome. Twardowski made great use of his new powers, riding round town on a gigantic rooster and showing the king a phantasm of his dead wife. To the chagrin of the Devil, Twardowski was a warm-hearted person and seemed to be doing more good than harm. The Devil arranged for a messenger to call him to an inn where a young woman was suffering a difficult childbirth. Twardowski realised this was a trap only when he got to the door and discovered that the inn was named 'Rome'. The Devil grabbed the magician and flew off into the night but Twardowski began to pray to the Virgin Mary, causing the Devil to drop him on the moon. He has stayed there ever since, his only companion a spider that sometimes dangles down on her web from the moon to catch the latest Krakow gossip and bring it back to her lonely master.

Kamienica Berowska

According to a relatively young legend (*c.*1890), this was the site of the fantastic banquet that Jan Długosz (writing in the late 15th century) claimed that a citizen named Wierzynek hosted in 1364 for the famous summit of kings. This brought together the monarchs of Poland (Kazimierz III the Great), Austria (Rudolf IV), the Holy Roman Empire and Bohemia (Charles IV), Cyprus (Peter de Lusignan), Denmark (Valdemar IV) and Hungary (Louis d'Anjou – later king of Poland too) with many princes to ensure peace in Central Europe. Legend states that the sumptuous banquet lasted 20 days and that Wierzynek handed out extravagant gifts, including golden spoons and plates.

Building on this impressive reputation, a restaurant named Pod Wierzynkiem was opened here in 1947. It was one of Krakow's few elegant restaurants for party functionaries and visiting diplomats for many years. Although there is no proof that the feast occurred on this spot, there is no proof that it did not – but it certainly was not in the current building, which replaced a wooden one in the latter half of the 15th century.
Rynek Główny 16.

Kamienica Gehanowska (Townhouse of the Gehan Family)

Built in the mid-14th century, this is a 'typical' Krakow *kamienica*. The café in the cellars preserves much old architecture (in spite of strange additions like a wall-sized mask) including an entry from the Rynek that is now over 2m (6ft) below the cobblestones. The

The Hetmańska bookshop

Pod Słońcem (Under the Sun) chemist did business from the 18th century until 1939 in what is now the antique shop. The café has taken up the name.
Rynek Główny 43.

Kamienica Hetmańska (Commander's Townhouse)

This very large, strategically-placed building was probably home to some dignitary when the square was laid out. By visiting the Da Pietro restaurant, you can see the 13th-century cellars. The ground floor contains a bookshop, whose remarkably well-preserved Gothic ribbed vaulting has rondels depicting knights' helms (one topped by a portrait of Kazimierz the Great). One very strange emblem near the centre of the ceiling shows three male faces whose beards grow into each other's hair. Even the bookshop is something of a monument: it has been here since 1796.
Rynek Główny 17 (the back entrance is from ul. Bracka 4).

Kamienica pod Obrazem (Townhouse Under the Picture)

Two smaller *kamienice* from the 14th and 15th centuries were combined to make this building. The gigantic icon of the Virgin Mary that covers much of the façade was probably added in 1718 by the Wentzl family whose ironmongery store filled the ground floor. At the beginning of the 20th century, the shop was turned into a restaurant, U Wentzla, and recently the upper storeys were renovated as a comfortable and elegant boutique hotel.
Rynek Główny 19.

Szara Kamienica (Grey Townhouse)

Legend claims that the building was named not from its colour but from one of Kazimierz the Great's many concubines, Sara, for whom he had it built. In the 19th century, it was owned by the Feintuch family of Jewish merchants. Marcin Feintuch converted to Christianity in 1846 and his son Stanisław took the surname Szarski, a rare case of a person named after a building and not the other way around. The Art Nouveau painter Mehoffer worked with the eclectic architect Talowski to create the beautiful interior of the Sklep Szarskiego (Szarski Shop), some of which survives in the restaurant that now fills the ground floor.
Rynek Główny 6.

Under the Picture and Wentzl Hotel

The Old University Campus

Jan Długosz wrote that, in founding the Academia Cracoviensis, King Kazimierz the Great 'wanted to augment and adorn his kingdom, just as other countries had done'. Founded in 1364, it was the 22nd university in Europe, and only the second 'east of the Rhine and north of the Alps' as the historian Karol Estreicher Jr put it.

The courtyard at Collegium Maius

The planned campus for Kazimierz the Great's *Academia* was in the town of Kazimierz, probably where the Jewish Quarter later stood. While waiting for buildings, law was taught on Wawel Hill and medicine in the homes of physicians. When the king died six years later, the campus remained unfinished and the new king, Louis the Hungarian was more interested in his own new university in Pecs. Abandoned and under-funded, the academy soon became little more than a name.

Louis's daughter Jadwiga, who became queen in 1384, showed more interest. She sent envoys to report on other universities and requested permission from the Pope to open a department of theology. When she died in 1399, she left all her gold and jewels to the academy. Her husband, King Władysław Jagiełło, re-founded it as the University of Krakow in 1400. Instead of keeping the university down in Kazimierz, Jagiełło and his successors bought out the Jewish Quarter in Old Town Krakow. The Jews were moved first to the area around today's Plac Szczepański and then to Kazimierz where, ironically, they ended up in the area probably first meant for the university.

In the 15th century, plenty of magnates and merchants were happy to endow *cathedrae* (professorial Chairs), *collegia* (professorial residences and lecture halls) or *bursae* (student residences). The university was especially famous for the sciences, which then included many things that would be considered 'magic' today. Astrology was one of the most prestigious and best-funded Chairs. Few professors of astrology are remembered today, but Nicolaus Copernicus (Mikołaj Kopernik, 1473–1543), who studied here during 1491–5, remains famous.

The medical school was known for alchemy, the magical arts of extending life and transforming base metals into gold. John Dee (1527–1608) and his assistant Edward Kelly, alchemists in Queen Elizabeth's court, came to consult their colleagues at Krakow in 1583. One of Europe's greatest alchemists, Sendivogius (Michał Sędziwój, 1566–1636) was based here. According to legend, Faust and Twardowski (*see p63*) were amongst those who came to drink from Krakow's font of forbidden wisdom.

In addition to sorcerers, the university produced many fine scientists, writers, lawyers, politicians and theologians. Jan III Sobieski (1629–96) remains one of the very few European monarchs who ruled with the benefit of a university education. Professor Karol Olszewski (1846–1915) was the first cryogenicist in the world to produce stable liquid oxygen and nitrogen. Karol Wojtyła (1920–2005) studied Polish literature before switching to theology and setting out on the road to becoming Pope John Paul II.

The university has outlived the Commonwealth Kingdom of Poland–Lithuania, the Free City of Krakow and the Austro-Hungarian Empire. In the 19th century, it was officially renamed the Jagiellonian University.

The university clock in Collegium Maius

Collegium Maius

The university's oldest building is Collegium Maius (Great College). The site was purchased in 1400 by King Jagiełło. Fragments of the large 14th-century limestone *kamienica* survive on the corner of ul. św. Anny and ul. Jagiellońska. Over the next 70 years, the university bought the remaining buildings on what was the Jewish market square and joined them together. In 1492–7 they were unified in Gothic style in red brick and pale limestone. The ambulatory (covered walkway) of the courtyard was typical of medieval universities, as was the projecting windowed balcony, designed to light the refectory lectern.

The building has been renovated many times. A particularly invasive 19th-century neo-Gothic makeover was undone by extensive surgery in the 1950s and 1960s. The Nazis plundered almost all the interiors, now mostly reconstructed from photographs using period artefacts from elsewhere.

The well at the centre of the courtyard (1958) shows the coats of arms of Krakow, Poland, Lithuania and Anjou. The 'Professors' Steps' run above the spot where treasure (presumably hidden by Jews) was found in 1494. It included a giant black diamond, which now adorns the reliquary containing St Stanisław's head in Wawel Cathedral.

At 11am and 1pm every day, the (modern) clock over the Golden Portal booms out the student hymn *Gaudeamus Igitur* and little figures from the university's history trundle around a walkway.

Muzeum Uniwersytetu Jagiellońskiego Collegium Maius (Jagiellonian University Museum, Collegium Maius)

Although much of the building is still in daily use, the middle floor serves as the university museum. Its treasures include royal sceptres, moon rock, an Oscar, a Nobel prize, the first globe to show North America and the astronomical instruments of Copernicus. There are rooms showing professors' lifestyles over the centuries and the ceremonial halls are still used to grant doctorates or greet visiting dignitaries.

The standard tour takes about 30 minutes and booking in advance is recommended. Tickets may be purchased in the office (entrance from the top floor of the courtyard). Times (and language) of tours vary from day to day so check when purchasing tickets on availability.
ul. Jagiellońska 15. Tel: (012) 663 1521. www.uj.edu.pl/muzeum. Open: Mon–Fri 11am–3pm, Sat 11am–2pm. Admission charge.

Ancient and modern sciences

Four rooms on the ground floor of Collegium Maius allow visitors to perform a few experiments of their own with interactive exhibits. Experiments with sound waves and astronomy sit alongside both computers and GPS. One room is solely dedicated to alchemy, with retorts, flasks, pots, magical diagrams, mysterious powders and dead animals. Tickets may be purchased at the gift shop opposite the entrance.
ul. Jagiellońska 15. Tel: (012) 422 1033, reservations (012) 663 1319. Open: Mon–Sat 10am–2.30pm.

Collegium Novum

The main administrative building dates only from 1883–7, hence 'New College'. Although there are no guided tours, you can wander the spacious halls during office hours (*Mon–Fri 10am–4pm*). If you are lucky, you might catch a conference or concert in the dazzling Aula Magna, possibly the finest neo-Gothic lecture hall in Europe. Its walls are hung with paintings of great scholars and kings. A large plaque outside is dedicated to the professors rounded up here by the Nazis on 6 November 1939 and sent to concentration camps during Sonderaktion Krakau. Although the Nazis intended to eradicate Polish learning, the professors who escaped continued to teach illegally in private houses.

Copernicus in a revolutionary mood

Collegium Nowodworskie

Built 1638–43 for the school associated with the university, since 1949 it has housed the Medical School. Although essentially early Baroque, it retained many features from medieval buildings, including the courtyard with ambulatory and open arcades.
ul. św. Anny 12.

Kościół św. Anny (St Ann's Church)

Replacing a Gothic church built by King Jagiełło in 1407, this collegiate church was erected 1689–1703 at the zenith of the Baroque style. Here all the important events on the university calendar are marked. The main altar is the Konfesja św. Jana Kantego (Confession of St John of Kanti), final resting place of a professor (1390–1473) who was made a saint in 1767. Other famous professors and students are remembered too. There is a monument to Copernicus in the transept and there are Turkish insignia captured at Vienna by Jan III Sobieski. Whenever a professor dies, the church is hung with black flags; the most renowned are commemorated with a plaque.

PLUS RATIO QUAM VIS

Many mottoes have appeared below the coat of arms granted by King Jagiełło to his university. Each rector used what he saw fit, even departments had their own, such as the Medical School's: *Saluti publicae*. In 1964, on the university's 600th anniversary, Professor Karol Estreicher chose a single motto. For a university that had survived the Nazis and was battling with the communists, it was a bold statement: *Plus ratio quam vis* ('Reason over force') – a quotation from the last pagan Roman poet, Maximinianus, a favourite of medieval students.

Collegium Novum, the bureaucratic headquarters of the Jagiellonian University

Walk: the University Quarter

Oldest and largest of Krakow's 17 universities, the Jagiellonian University has nearly 40,000 students and hundreds of buildings across the city. After its re-founding in 1400 it dominated Old Town between ul. Bracka and ul. Szewska, sometimes referred to as 'the first campus'.

Allow 45 minutes.

Begin the walk where ul. św. Anny crosses the Planty gardens.

1 ul. św. Anny (St Anne's Street) and Kościół św. Anny (St Anne's Church)
The line of the old walls is shown in flagstones on the inner edge of the Planty gardens. Where ul. św. Anny crosses that line, a small postern gate served as entrance to the oldest Jewish Quarter in Krakow from at least 1300 until 1470.

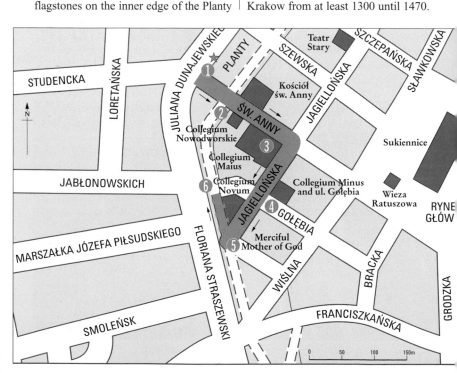

The Jewish cemetery was somewhere on the far side of the moat from the postern. 'Jewish Street' was renamed 'St Anne's Street' (after the church) when the Jews began to move north to the area around Plac Szczepański. Their buildings were bought by the growing Jagiellonian University. Take a peek into the Baroque church on your left (*see p69*), which contains souvenirs of students who became saints, kings or astronomers. *Walk back across the street to the building opposite.*

2 Collegium Nowodworskie

This university building has no special provision for tourists, but you may visit its graceful Baroque courtyard. Originally a secondary school associated with the university (*see p69*), the building is a blend of medieval college traditions with newer fashions in art. Note the gate (usually locked) leading from this courtyard into the next. The Rector's Law was binding inside the university campus while Town Law was binding outside. Students who were fugitives from Town Law could safely move between university buildings via these gates. *Return to ul. św. Anny, turning right. Follow the street to the first corner, and turn right into ul. Jagiellońska.*

3 Collegium Maius

King Jagiełło ordered the purchase of a large *kamienica*, which became Collegium Maius (Great College) in 1400 (*see p67*).

4 Collegium Minus and ul. Gołębia

At the corner of ul. Jagiellońska and ul. Gołębia is Collegium Minus (Lesser College), built *c.*1462 and extended several times since. It is now the home of the archaeology department. The narrow canyon of ul. Gołębia, opposite, was the site of many university *collegia* and *bursae*. All sorts of infamy could be found here in the 15th and 16th centuries. Duelling was popular, even though it was illegal. The students, who were expected to live priestly lives, somehow managed to run everything from taverns to brothels from their halls of residence. *Continue straight down ul. Jagiellońska to the end.*

5 The Merciful Mother of God and the Planty

The Baroque statue of the Merciful Mother of God originally stood in Plac Mariacki at the entrance to the graveyard (*see pp30 31*). When that was decommissioned by the Habsburg authorities in the 18th century, the statue was moved to ul. Kapucyńska. It arrived here during the Second World War. *Turn right to follow the Planty.*

6 Collegium Novum

Walking along the Planty, you can see the line of the walls again in the flagstones. The neo-Gothic Collegium Novum (New College, built 1883–7, *see p68*) extends over the medieval walls and the site of Baszta Miechowników (Bellows-Makers' Tower). The tree in front of the building was planted in 1919 to mark the first anniversary of Polish independence. Nearby is a statue of Copernicus holding an astrolabe.

The year 1241 brought terrible destruction to Krakow, when the Tartar hordes burnt and looted everything beyond the safety of Wawel's mighty ramparts and St Andrew's fortified church. Construction began a new phase in 1257 when a town square and streets were laid out in a regular grid covering roughly 120 acres (0.5sq km). The events of 1241 and 1257 bracket the final forms of Romanesque in Krakow and the beginnings of Gothic.

The religious orders that had arrived earlier in the 13th century, the Dominicans, Franciscans and Cistercians, became fashion leaders in importing architectural styles at the end of the century. Amongst others, the Franciscan Church (*see pp41–2*) on ul. Franciszkańska and the Dominican church at the far end of Plac Wszystkich Świętych introduced the style to Old Town after the Tartar invasion. Their layout is typical of medium-sized early Gothic churches. They are built of red brick with a few accents in local limestone, which became the material of choice for nearly all Krakow's Gothic churches.

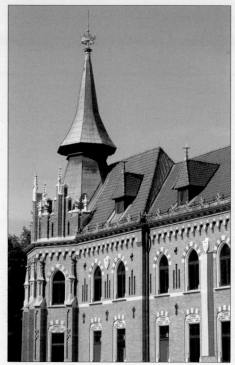

The reign of King Kazimierz III the Great (1310–70) was a rich flowering of both religious and secular Gothic architecture. Under his patronage, the loose collection of Romanesque buildings on Wawel Hill was integrated into a powerful castle complex, of which a few fragments are still visible (mostly towers and the lower levels of the castle, *see pp84–5*). The municipal buildings on Rynek Główny were rebuilt in a style befitting the trade centre of a prosperous economy. The arches of Kazimierz's Sukiennice, the equivalent of the Stock Exchange in its day, are still visible under the later Renaissance layers, and the chambers of the Town Hall Tower once housed the debates of the powerful burghers of the Town Council (see p35). Nearby, Kamienica Hetmańska (the Commander's Townhouse) preserves a bas-relief portrait of King Kazimierz in a ceiling that was probably carved shortly after his death (see pp64–5).

King Kazimierz also patronised the building or renovation of Krakow's largest and most important churches. Whereas architects in the West were moving towards paper-thin walls and stained glass, held together with flying buttresses, Kazimierz's architects were constrained by Krakow's tight urban planning and developed an alternative scheme of long, thin churches with buttresses close to the walls. Kościół Mariacki (see pp43–5) and the Wawel Cathedral (see pp80–82) were renovated in this style and the new churches of St Catherine's (see pp99–100) and Corpus Christi (see p99) were built for the town of Kazimierz.

The final phase of Gothic art in Krakow developed in the late 15th century as the Renaissance was already blooming in Italy. Nuremberg-born Wit Stwosz (1438–1533) raised sculpture to new levels of expressiveness in masterpieces such as the Mariacki altarpiece (see p44) and the disturbing restlessness of the tomb of Kazimierz IV the Jagiellonian (see p82). Although

Stwosz returned to his native city in about 1492, his influence was visible for many years afterwards in Cracovian artists who had learned their trade in his workshop.

The 15th century also saw the spread of practical gunpowder weapons and the consequent loss of importance for mounted knights. King Jan I 'Olbracht' (1459–1501) ordered the building of new fortifications in keeping with developments in warfare. High walls became less important than keeping many lines of fire open to the defenders, and complex shapes like Krakow's picturesque barbican (see p28) appeared.

Opposite: Gothic architecture
Above: The tomb of Kazimierz IV

Palaces

As the former capital of Poland, Krakow has many noblemens' homes whose main purpose was to demonstrate the wealth and power of aristocratic families to their jealous neighbours. Although many fell into disrepair over the centuries, some were renovated in the 1990s and returned to public service.

King Kazimierz the Great

Krakow has 87 palaces and stately manors of the nobility. Most of the palaces inside the Old Town walls were built on a ground plan roughly twice the size of a standard *kamienica* (*see p62*). Those outside the walls could afford spacious gardens and subsidiary buildings.

KING KAZIMIERZ THE GREAT

The last king of the Piast dynasty, Kazimierz III (1310–70) came to the Polish throne in 1333. He was already known to his contemporaries as 'the Great' for his unusual height but quickly went on to earn the name in other fields as well. He built 80 castles, fortified 20 cities and extended Poland's borders to nearly twice their previous length. Later historians quipped that 'Kazimierz the Great received a Poland made of wood but gave it back built of stone'. He codified Polish law and founded Poland's first university. His even-handed justice, not just for the nobility but for peasants and Jews as well, became proverbial.

Kazimierz was also a man of great physical appetites. He was known for his mighty feasts at which he consumed prodigious amounts of food and drink. He had four more-or-less consecutive wives (he managed to have two at once for a few months), two fiancées who never became wives and at least two well-documented mistresses – but many, many more in court gossip and legend. His most famous love affair was supposedly with a beautiful Jewish girl named Esther. According to legend, their daughters were raised in Judaism and their two sons as Christian princes. Fearing that her time in the king's favour was coming to an end, Esther committed suicide by jumping out of a window of the Łobzów Palace.

Unfortunately, the one thing that Kazimierz the Great could not do was produce a male heir. He had three illegitimate sons by mistresses but his wives produced only daughters. After his death, the crown passed to his nephew, King Louis d'Anjou the Hungarian.

Pałac Biskupi (Bishop's Palace)

The official residence of Krakow's bishops. The first palace on this spot was raised some time before 1384 but burnt down in the 15th century. It was rebuilt several times in several styles, fragments of which can be found in odd leftovers, such as Gothic and Renaissance portals. By the 17th century it had something like its current look. Under the Austro-Hungarian Empire, the Bishop's Palace functioned as a sort of unofficial museum of Polish history. It was the residence of Archbishop Karol Wojtyła (later Pope John Paul II) from 1963 to 1978. A plaque by the door commemorates his first visit to Poland after his election and a statue of him raising his arms in blessing stands in the courtyard.

ul. Franciszkańska 3. Trams: 1, 2, 8, 18.

Pałac Pod Baranami (Palace Under the Sign of the Rams)

This building was already known in the 16th century as Sub Agnes after a sculpture on the building that showed a single ram's head on the corner shared by two ram's bodies, one on each wall. From across either street, it gave the impression of a single, normal ram. From the corner, however, it was a fantastic monster.

The palace belonged to a succession of kings, princes and the wealthiest Polish nobility, who brought in all the latest fashions from Italy and France. The original rams were removed by subsequent renovations, but the name stuck and the early 19th-century Classicist façade brought them back, this time as three rams' heads over the entrance.

In 1960, the cellars became the home of one of the most famous cabarets in Poland, the Piwnica Pod Baranami (*see p154*). Alumni of the cabaret have continued to dominate the cultural life of Krakow, even after the death of its leader Piotr Skrzynecki in 1997.

Rynek Główny 27.

Pałac Pugetów is now a business centre

Pałac Pugetów (Puget Palace)

Built during 1874–5 for Baron Konstanty de Puget, its transplanted neo-Renaissance Parisian style is not found anywhere else in Krakow. The de Pugets had moved to Poland from France in the 18th century and it seems the baron was emphasising his family

The Bishop's Palace was once the home of Pope John Paul II

roots when he asked the (Polish) architect to design something so emphatically French. Today, the palace houses upmarket business offices with an art gallery in the cellar. True Cracovians still pronounce the 'g' in Pugetów as in French (soft 'zh'), but outsiders use Polish hard 'g'.
ul. Starowiślna 13.

Pałac Wielopolskich (Wielopolskich Palace)

This building has served as Krakow's Town Hall since the Gothic edifice on Rynek Główny was torn down in the 19th century. The early 16th-century Renaissance palace was owned by various aristocratic families before belonging to the Wielopolskie family about 1650.

In the 1850s, the Viennese Winter's Kaffeehaus was opened here. It was the place to see and be seen for the upper crust of Galician Krakow. They added a ballroom, where dashing cavalry officers could waltz with fluttering countesses, and a glassed-in patio in front of the building where a baron could take in the morning papers while sipping his coffee. In honour of the Crown Prince's birthday in 1854, the coffee house was the first building in Krakow to use electric lighting.

When the city purchased the palace in 1864, the porch was removed and the figures of Labour and Dignity were set to guard the entrance to the building. Where polite society once danced the night away, politicians now argue over new sewage systems and tram tracks. There are no tours of the building but it is easy to wander around if you look as if you have some business there.
Pl. Wszystkich Świętych 3.

Willa Decjusza (Villa Decius)

Justus Decjusz the Elder (Ludwig Jodok Dietz, *c.*1485–1545) was an Alsatian German Humanist who started his career in Poland by helping to pay off the dowry of an Italian queen. He gave his first name to the district of Wola

Justowska (earlier known as Wola Chełmska) and his surname to the palace that he built in the 1630s, Willa Decjusza (Decius' Villa). He gave both names to his son, Justus Decjusz the Younger (c.1520–67), who propagated Calvinism in Poland, using the villa's grounds for Protestant prayer meetings.

The charming Renaissance palace is now administered by a private foundation that has painstakingly renovated the main palace and outlying buildings. It serves as Krakow's most elegant conference centre and houses a chic restaurant in the cellars.
ul. Kasztanowa 1. Bus: 134.

Willa Decjusza in Wola Justowska

Only one of Krakow's many medieval churches escaped a Baroque makeover and many Gothic *kamienicy* now have ostentatious Baroque entrance portals.

The Jesuits brought Baroque architecture with them from Rome. The new style emphasised the emotional side of religion. Acoustics became significant in church design as the importance of the sermon grew. New allegorical motifs, such as the 'wheel of death' in St Catherine's church (*see pp99–100*), supplemented the sermon as carriers of moral truth.

The first king of the Vasa dynasty in Poland, Zygmunt III, had been educated by the Jesuits and was a wholehearted supporter of their ideological and aesthetic programmes. He funded Kościół św. Piotra i Pawła (Sts Peter and Paul, *see p46*), which in 1597 became the first full-blown example of the new Roman style north of the Alps. Based on Il Gesu, the headquarters church of the Jesuit Order, the Cracovian church was an exemplar of the basic pattern of early Baroque churches – a spacious cross-shaped floor plan with a cupola over the meeting-point of the two axes. Departing from the medieval tradition, it had no towers.

However, at the start of the 17th century, Lombard architect Andrea Spezza (c.1580–1628) re-integrated flanking towers into the new Jesuit-style façade at the Camaldolese monastery church at Bielany (*see p142*), introducing a variant that became a hallmark of the local style.

The masters of this early period were almost exclusively imported from Italy. The royal architect, Giovanni Battista Trevano (c.1570–1643), updated the Wawel Castle, designed St Stanisław's ebullient tomb and oversaw the final stages of the building of Sts Peter and Paul in which he tried to harmonise the Italian design with local forms. Giovanni Battista Falconi's workshop produced stucco work to decorate the interior of Sts Peter and Paul as well as the monastic church at Bielany. Trevano worked on the design of Isaac's Synagogue, and Falconi's stucco adorned the ceiling (*see pp102–03*).

Under the reign of their alumnus, King Jan III Sobieski, the professors of the Jagiellonian University were able to build a church to equal that of their rivals, the Jesuits. Designed by the Italian-educated Dutchman, Tilman van Gameren (1632–1706), the collegiate church of St Anne's (started in 1680)

Bilet wstępu do Kopalni Soli w Wieliczce

• Trasa Turystyczna • Muzeum Żup Krakowskich

Grupowy - normalny

771946

1978 - 2003 25 lat na Pierwszej Liście Światowego Dziedzictwa Kulturalnego i Naturalnego UNESCO
1978 - 2003 25 Years on UNESCO's First List of World Cultural and Natural Heritage

W Kopalni Soli w Wieliczce organizujemy:

- konferencje, bankiety, koncerty śluby w kaplicy św. Kingi, hale, biesiady górnicze...
- pobyty w podziemnym ośrodku rehabilitacyjno - leczniczym
- w sezonie jesienno - zimowym atrakcyjne imprezy dla dzieci

The Salt Mine in Wieliczka organizes:

- conferences, banquets, concerts, wedding ceremonies at St. Kinga's Chapel, miner's revels...
- sojourns in the underground rehabilitation and treatment centre
- attractive events for children during autumn and winter

Kopalnia Soli „Wieliczka" Trasa Turystyczna sp. z o.o.

ul. Daniłowicza 10, 32-020 Wieliczka, Polska; tel. (+48 12) 278 73 66, 278 73 02; www.kopalnia.pl

borrowed fresh Roman models as well as local developments such as the flanking towers at Bielany. St Anne's is a fine example of the Cracovian tendency to combine rather austere exteriors with sumptuous interiors. The interior decoration of St Anne's is largely the work of Baldassare Fontana (1661–1733), an Italian in Bernini's circle. Fontana's sculptures and stucco defy the limitations of their construction. The frenzied climax of his style can be seen up close in the ceilings in Dom Pod Gruszką (now a restaurant), which resemble a very large wedding cake thrown violently at the ceiling.

By the end of the Baroque period, radical changes had taken hold in Krakow. Royal patronage for the arts and construction dwindled when the court moved to Warsaw. Wars, plagues and famine had reduced the city's population and emptied the coffers of the burghers. On the other hand, the Roman Catholic Church was enjoying renewed prosperity. In the new climate of popular piety, Krakow's churches and their generous roster of saints had become a lucrative pilgrimage destination. The proceeds were used to build new churches and to give unfashionable Romanesque and Gothic churches cosmetic makeovers. Kacper Bażanka (c.1680–1726) was a Pole whose studies in Rome inspired many innovations. His renovation of 'Na Skałce' (see p100) and the new construction of the Kościół Pijarów (see p45) introduced the Roman model of churches that seas off the end of a street, an idea alien to the medieval town layouts of Krakow and Kazimierz. He was also an important exponent of *quadrattura*, the use of *trompe-l'œil* to extend the apparent size of buildings.

As Baroque began to transform into Classicism and Rococo, money and power were flowing north to Warsaw. Many Cracovian churches remained frozen in the styles of earlier centuries. Francesco Placidi (c.1710–82) was one of the last great architects of the Baroque tradition to work in Krakow. The best example of this phase is his façade of the Kościół Pijarów (see p45), which updated Bażanka's design to Enlightenment tastes.

Opposite: The church of Sts Peter and Paul
Below: A Baroque portal on ul. Stradom

The Dragon's bones
outside Wawel Cathedral

Wawel Hill

Writing about Wawel in its days of ignominy, when an Austro-Hungarian garrison was quartered in the castle of Polish kings, Wyspiański claimed 'Here everything is Poland, every stone and every crumb, and the man who enters here becomes a part of Poland … Around you is Poland, the eternal'.

Wawel has often been called the 'the Polish Acropolis' as well as 'the Polish Necropolis'. It has even recently been elevated by some to the title of a 'Chakra of the Earth'. It is Poland's most important storehouse of national identity and it will take the visitor a long time to unpack all its treasures.

The Zygmunt funerary chapel

It is best to start a visit to Wawel in the morning. Most of its buildings close about 3pm and, in summer and on school holidays, tickets sometimes sell out for the more popular attractions. On Mondays, many of them are closed, except in summer. Each ticket shows the entry time that you are expected to enter each site. Although it may lead to mild panic as you rush to the next exhibit, it does avoid long queues. You can call ahead (*tel: (012) 422 1697*) to reserve tickets but they may not speak English and they will usually tell you there is no need to reserve tickets (even if they are likely to sell out before you arrive!). English-speaking certified guides are also available.

Katedra św. Stanisława (St Stanislaus' Cathedral)
The Wawel Cathedral was the shrine of the monarchs of Poland and the nobles of their courts. Even after the capital moved to Warsaw in the 17th century, kings still returned here for coronation and, at the end of their reigns, for burial beside their predecessors.

The first cathedral was built on this spot shortly after AD 1000, when the first bishop of Krakow was consecrated.

After a Bohemian attack damaged it, a new Romanesque building was built under the patronage of Prince Władysław Herman around the turn of the 11th and 12th centuries. Although most of the church burnt down in 1306, the Crypt of St Leonard remains. The basic structure of the current church is from the Gothic building consecrated in 1364, under King Kazimierz the Great. However, every generation has added something to the building, making it seem like an encyclopaedia of Polish architecture through the ages.

Hanging to the right of the main entrance into the Cathedral, three large bones are suspended by a chain. According to legend, they are the dragon's bones (*see p89*) and if they should ever fall from their chains, the world will come to an end. (The chains are regularly replaced with new ones, just in case.)

The clock on Wawel Cathedral

According to palaeontologists, the bones seem to come from extinct species of rhinoceros, mammoth and whale.

The central shrine with its Baroque marble-and-gold canopy is the final resting place of Bishop Stanisław (Stanislaus) of Szczepanowo (*c.*1030–79), canonised in 1253 to become the patron saint of Poland. Known as Konfesja św. Stanisława (a 'confession' was the burial place of early Christian martyrs), the current version of the altar was built in 1626–9, probably by Trevano. The silver casket now contains not only the remains of St Stanisław, but also pieces of St Florian that were moved here from Kościół św. Floriana. This altar was the place where triumphant Polish kings laid the spoils of war. The main altar of the Cathedral, further into the church, is a much more subdued affair.

In the aisle to the right of the Confession, the canopied tombs of Kazimierz III the Great (1310–70) and Władysław II Jagiełło (1351–1434) depict those mighty lieges in red marble, lying placidly at rest. Between them, Queen Jadwiga (1374–99), wife of Jagiełło, also has a white marble sepulchre (made in 1902) but her mortal remains were moved to a silver reliquary after she became a saint in 1997. The royal insignia from her tomb are on display in a nearby glass case. The cathedral also contains a miraculous crucifix (late 13th century) that 'made conversation' – as the Latin says – with the Sainted Queen.

The nave of the cathedral is surrounded by a number of chapels. Kaplica Świętokrzyska (Holy Cross

Chapel), just to the right of the entrance, was erected towards the end of the 15th century. The bosses in the Gothic ceiling show the coats of arms of Lithuania, Poland and Hungary, and heavenly choirs sing in the almost eastern-looking frescoes between the ribs of the ceiling. Among the graves in the chapel is the amazing tomb of Kazimierz IV the Jagiellonian. In sharp contrast with the restful images of the other kings, his – carved by Wit Stwosz out of red- and white-flecked marble about 1492 – shows him writhing on his deathbed.

Kaplica Zygmuntowska (Chapel of the Zygmunts), built in 1519–33, is one of the most important and influential monuments of the Renaissance in Poland and is often claimed as the finest of its sort north of Italy. The golden dome on the exterior of the chapel is repeated by the Kaplica Wazów

immediately next to it and its influence can be seen in Kościół św. Piotra i Pawła (*see p46*). The rich interior set the standard for the next century of funerary chapels throughout the kingdom. It is particularly notable for the stunning contrast between the white sandstone and highly polished red marble. Between the graves of Zygmunts I and II and the formidable Queen Anna Jagiellonka (1523–96), there are depictions of Old Testament kings and the Four Evangelists.

Kaplica Wazów (Chapel of the Vasas) was built in 1664–76 on what may have been the site of a Romanesque chapel to hold St Stanisław's bones. This mausoleum for the Vasa dynasty was designed to parallel the Kaplica Zygmuntowska of their predecessors. Its black marble and golden angels give this Baroque shrine a very sombre quality.

You do not need a ticket to view most of the Cathedral, which is open to the public from sunrise to sunset. Dzwon Zygmunt and Groby Królewskie require tickets that must be bought in one of the kiosks near the entrances to Wawel.

Dzwon Zygmunt (The Zygmunt Bell)

An old joke went 'When the Zygmunt Bell rings at Christmas, you can hear it up to Easter'. The joke is that Wielkanoc (Easter) was a village just outside Krakow. Nonetheless, at 2.5m (8ft) in diameter and nearly 11 tons, the Zygmunt Bell is very loud. Since cracks showed up in the clapper, however, the bell has been saved for special occasions. According to a legend known to every schoolchild who climbs the steep steps

The Zygmunt Bell

to the tower, if you ring the bell your wish will come true. The view alone is well worth the climb. You need a ticket to enter the tower. *Open: Mon–Sat 9am–3pm, Sun 12.15–3pm.*

Groby Królewskie (Royal Tombs)

These labyrinthine crypts contain a rather long list of dead Polish monarchs. For those without an intimate knowledge of royal genealogy, the most important part of the tour will probably be the simple beauty of the Romanesque Crypt of St Leonard. The crypt is a fragment of the cathedral started by Prince Władysław Herman in the 1090s.

Also buried here are Generals Poniatowski and Kościuszko, who fought revolutions on two continents, and 20th-century leaders of Poland, Marshal Piłsudski and General Sikorski. You need a ticket to enter the Royal Tombs. *Open: Mon–Fri 9am–7.15pm, Sat 9am–4.45pm, Sun 12.30–5.15pm.*

Krypta Wieszczów Narodowych (Crypt of National Bards)

Two great Polish Romantic poets lie buried here: Adam Mickiewicz (1798–1855) and Juliusz Słowacki (1809–49). Both devoted their entire literary output to the memory of Poland, at a time when it had been wiped from the map. By keeping alive a sense of national identity, they fulfilled a role every bit as important as kings; their interment here, close to the Royal Graves, is a recognition of that. Tickets are not required to visit the Crypt of National Bards.

Muzeum Katedralne (Cathedral Museum)

The Museum (founded by Karol Wojtyła, the late Pope John Paul II) contains a selection from the cathedral's centuries of tradition. One of the stranger items on display is a spearhead known as the Lance of St Maurice, claimed to be the one that pierced Jesus' side at the crucifixion. It was given to King Bolesław I by the Holy Roman Emperor Otto III and is nearly identical to another in Vienna that fascinated young Adolf Hitler as the 'Spear of Destiny'. No-one knows whether the one in Vienna is the original, but Krakow's is almost certainly a copy. A few display cases are also dedicated to odds and ends of

Atmospheric crypts abound

Hussar feathered armour

Wojtyła's life in Krakow. *Open: Mon–Sat 9am–3pm, Sun 12.30–3pm.*

Smocza Jama (The Dragon's Den)

You enter this limestone cave by 135 steps winding down from the level of the castle courtyard, but the exit is near the river. Unless you intend to climb back up the hill, save this site for the end of your visit to Wawel. Although the 50m (164ft) tourist track through this small hole in the limestone rock is well-lit and the walkway is smooth, the most interesting features are unmarked. Near the start, a grille set into the right-hand wall stops tourists from wandering another 80m (295ft) into the hill, since the cave is underwater in places. Further along, a mysterious human burial from the 17th century was discovered. At that time, the cave served as a wine cellar

for a boisterous bordello and it is possible that the body was buried here to avoid inconvenient questions from the authorities after a brawl. The final section of the cave shows the 18th-century brickwork of the fortifications designed by Kościuszko. Just outside the den is the dragon himself in the form of a sculpture by Bronisław Chromy (1963). During the warmer months, a gas jet inside the dragon's mouth bursts into flame once a minute. *Open: 1 May–31 Oct, daily 10am–5pm.*

Wawel Zaginiony (Lost Wawel)

This strange and interesting exhibit takes you on walkways under the floors of the castle kitchens but above the level of older buildings that have been unearthed. One of the most important fragments is the lower part of an early-Romanesque rotunda church. Glass cases feature the remains of everyday life on Wawel Hill as recovered from various archaeological digs as well as models of what Wawel looked like at various stages. *Open: 1 Nov–31 Mar, Sun 10am–3pm, Mon 9.30am–noon, Tue–Fri 9.30am–4pm, Sat 9.30am–3pm.*

Zamek Królewski (Royal Castle)

The first castle on this spot was presumably a wooden fortress of the Wiślan tribe, surrounded by earthworks and palisade walls. Its outlines are lost, even to archaeology, amongst the many layers of building and rebuilding in later centuries. Kazimierz I the Restorer moved his court here in 1038, making Krakow the capital of the young Polish kingdom. Kazimierz III the Great rebuilt the Romanesque buildings into a massive Gothic castle complex. Zygmunt I the Old rebuilt it in Renaissance style and Trevano introduced many Baroque elements.

The motto over the entrance to the castle reads: *Si Deus nobiscum, quis contra nos?* (If God is with us, who is against us?) Passing through the dark tunnel leads into the bright castle courtyard with its stunning, three-tiered Renaissance colonnade by Bartolomeo Berrecci (1480–1537). From the courtyard, you may enter four sections of the castle.

Reprezentacyjne Komnaty Królewskie (Royal State Rooms)

Fires and plundering armies destroyed most of the original interiors of the

The bell tower at Wawel Cathedral

Wawel Castle. The reconstructions on display are mostly extrapolations from surviving fragments, borrowings from less-devastated buildings or plausible inventions based on contemporary descriptions. Many private citizens donated family heirlooms, both after the Austro-Hungarian Army decommissioned the castle in 1906 (it had served as a barracks) and again after the Nazi looting during the Second World War.

The Royal State Rooms are on the top storey. They represent the portions of the castle that courtiers and dignitaries would have visited most often. They are designed to impress both with their size and the richness of their decoration. The Sala Poselska (Deputies' Hall) contains one of the most famous treasures of Polish art, the 'Wawel Heads'. Originally, 194 human heads and 5 coats of arms carved out of plane wood looked down on the deputies from the ceiling. It was probably intended as an allegory of a whole society united under the rule of King Zygmunt I the Old. Created by Sebastian Tauerbach, it was completed about 1540.

The original ceiling was pulled down by the Austro-Hungarian Army in the 19th century, when they converted the building into a barracks. About 20 of the heads were saved by noble Polish families as keepsakes of past glory. During reconstruction in the 1920s, a new, coffered ceiling in a Renaissance style was built and 30 of the original heads were donated by their owners.

One of the heads is that of a woman with a gag over her mouth. Legend claims that a poor widow was unjustly accused of theft by one of the burghers and brought before King Zygmunt Augustus for sentencing. The king was more inclined to believe the rich merchant than the poor widow and ordered her to be flogged. One of the sculptures on the ceiling suddenly spoke out in her defence: *Rex Auguste iudice iuste!* (August king, be just in judgement!). The shocked king rescinded his sentence but also ordered the sculpture to be gagged so that similar incidents could not happen again.

This level of the castle contains some of the Arrasy Zygmuntowskie (Zygmunt

The exit from the Dragon's cave

Tapestries). They are in three major thematic series: the Book of Genesis, Animals and Landscapes, and Grotesques (mostly monograms and coats of arms entwined with allegorical or mythological figures). The tapestries, in various shapes and sizes, were tailor-made for specific places on the castle walls. The largest ones illustrate the Book of Genesis, including the Story of Noah. This set, thanks to detailed contemporary descriptions, has been arranged in the Sala Senatorska (Senators' Hall) as it was first hung for the marriage of Zygmunt II the August to Catherine of Austria in 1553.

In 1795, the tapestries were taken to Russia on the orders of Catherine the Great. They were returned in 1921, thanks to the Treaty of Riga that ended the Polish-Bolshevik War. At the start of the Second World War they were smuggled out to Canada but did not return until 1961. *Open: 1 Nov–31 Mar, Tue–Sat 9.30am–3pm, Sun 10am–3pm; 1 Apr–31 Oct, as above but Mon 9.30am–3pm, Tue and Fri open until 4pm.*

Prywatne Apartamenty Królewskie (Royal Private Apartments)
The Royal Private Apartments on the middle storey of the castle are generally lower and less flamboyant than the State Rooms. They include bedrooms and offices for the royal family and important court officers. More of the Arrasy Zygmuntowskie are on display here, especially medium-sized tapestries in the Animals and Landscapes series. *Open: same as State Rooms except closed on Mon.*

Skarbiec i Zbrojownia (Treasury and Armoury)

The Treasury section contains the coronation insignia of the Kingdom of Poland. One of the most important exhibits is the coronation sword Szczerbiec, the notched sword. Legend claims that King Bolesław I the Brave (c. 966–1025) notched the blade of the sword when he struck the Golden Gate of Kiev. The legend is made unlikely by the style of the sword, which suggests it was forged in the early 13th century. Nonetheless, it is an outstanding example of medieval craftsmanship and is the only item of the Piast dynasty insignia that continued to be used in later centuries.

The Armoury is a king-sized collection of things to kill people with. There are racks of crossbows, muskets, halberds, axes, swords and spears and rows of cannon and hussar armour. Some of the odder items are the weapons that combine more than one function, such as the hunter's dirk that has a built-in flintlock pistol that shoots along the blade. *Open: daily 9.30am–3pm except Mon 9.30am–noon, Tue & Fri 9.30am–4pm, Sun 10am–3pm.*

Sztuka Wschodu (Art of the Orient)

This collection of oddments includes trophies of war, diplomatic gifts from far-off monarchs and trade goods. The only thing that holds them together is that they are from the Orient – from Turkey to Japan. There are carpets, tents, flags, saddles and porcelain. In several places you can see contrasting architectural styles in the walls, including pieces of King Kazimierz III's

Gothic fortress. *Open: 1 Nov–31 Mar, Tue–Sat 9.30am–3pm, Sun 10am–3pm; 1 April–31 Oct, as above but Tue and Fri open until 4pm.*

The Chakra

After you enter the courtyard, the chakra (*see p91*) is reputed to be near the corner of the courtyard immediately to your left. The castle administration, which has an almost irrational hatred for the legend of the chakra, has now taken down the unintentionally humorous sign that explained that there is no chakra on this spot. Instead, they 'subtly' leave all sorts of scaffolding and signs up against the wall to make it difficult for meditators to get at their favourite energy currents. Do not ask certified guides about the chakra; they are not allowed to discuss it.

Display at the Armoury

Walk: Wawel, the Polish Acropolis

On Wawel, you may get lost among all the kings, wars and borders, but its majesty and beauty speak for themselves.

Allow 1 hour just to look around but 3 or 4 if you want to visit the exhibits.

Start at the foot of Wawel Hill, near the end of ul. Kanonicza.

1 Wawel Bricks and Herbowa Brama

Walking up the ramp, notice the Wawel Bricks – red or inscribed grey – from the 1921–36 renovation: 6,329 were sponsored, but only 1,800 were made and 788 can still be seen.

The gate on the hill – Herbowa Brama (Coat-of-Arms Gate) – was built in 1921. On your left is the Tower of Władysław IV: he renovated it in 1644–6 but it dates from 1581. The monument to Kościuszko (hero of the American Revolution and Polish Uprisings) is a copy of the 1921

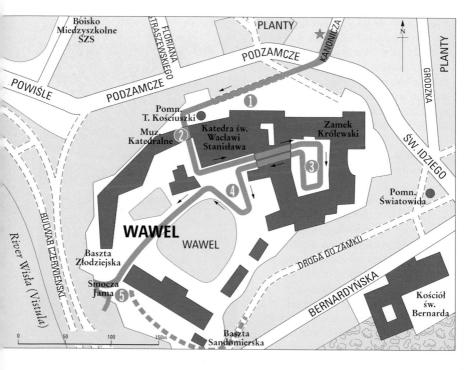

original, destroyed by the Nazis.
Wawel was headquarters of Hans Frank,
Governor-General of Poland. To your
right is a ticket office for entry to Wawel.

2 Brama Wazów (Vasa Gate) and Cathedral

Vasa Gate, once the only entrance, is
decorated with the Polish (white eagle)
and Vasa (wheatsheaf) coats of arms. To
the right is the Cathedral Museum (*see
p83*), to the left is the Cathedral
(*see pp80–81*). The Dragon's bones hang
by the entrance. Turn and follow the
Cathedral wall, noticing the many
architectural styles, especially the twin
cupolas of Kaplica Zygmuntowska
(Chapel of the Zygmunts) and Kaplica
Wazów (Chapel of the Vasas).
*Continue past the Cathedral, into the
passage ahead.*

3 Inner Courtyard

Pass under the green triumphal arch
into Berrecci's 16th-century courtyard.
The serenity and balance of its triple
colonnades may explain why some
people sense here a supernatural
source of unusual energy.
Wander back to the outer courtyard.

4 Outer Courtyard Gardens

Here was the 'upper city', which fell into
disrepair and was pulled down in the early
19th century. In 1846, Wawel became
Austrian barracks and the last buildings in
the outer courtyard were levelled for the
Grosser Parade Platz. Foundations of the
churches of St George and St Michael
were uncovered post-1945.
*Walk towards the gap in the encircling
walls.*

5 Dragon's Den

Walking between Baszta Złodziejska
(Thieves' Tower) and the Austro-
Hungarian military hospital (now
a plush restaurant), you come to a
triangular platform overlooking the
Wisła. At its point is a bartizan over
a dried-up well. In season (1 May–
31 October), you may descend by stairs
inside the well into the Dragon's Den
(*see p84*). The exit is by the river.
Otherwise, continue past the hospital,
by Baszta Sandomierska (Sandomierz
Tower), built for cannons in the 15th
century on a Romanesque base –
supposedly Sandomierz noblemen
helped pay for it – to Brama
Bernardyńska (Bernardine Gate),
built in the 1940s and named after
the Bernardine monastery below.
*From here it is a short walk to
Kazimierz (see p98) or Old Town.*

The Cathedral on Wawel Hill is a mixture of
many architectural styles

The Cracovian penchant for legend manifests itself in scores of stories about Wawel, not all ancient.

The Dragon

Once upon a time, King Krak of the Wiślanie started to build a castle on the limestone rock of Wawel. This disturbed the slumbers of a dragon in the cave underneath, Smocza Jama (Dragon's Den). He began to eat sheep, cattle and virgins, as dragons do. The wise king invited brave knights to slay the dragon for the usual rewards and they, of course, failed. Then a clever cobbler filled a sheepskin with sulphur and salt, sewed it up to look like a sheep, placed it outside the cave and made bleating noises until the dragon gobbled it up. The desperate dragon drank too much water and died.

This legend was first written down in the 13th century, when there was no cobbler and the monster wasn't a dragon. A similar story is told about Brno, in Moravia, and in Russia. It isn't clear who borrowed from whom. The dragon has become Krakow's unofficial mascot, in everything from cartoons to toys, recognisable to every Polish citizen – like the Lajkonik (*see p118*) and Pan Twardowski (*see p63*).

The name 'Krakow' (Krak's Settlement) suggests that a real Krak once ruled the city. The dragon may be left over from a pagan myth or symbolise the defeated old Slavic religion. Wawel had a church of St Michael (usually depicted trampling a dragon) in the 11th century; St George the Dragon-Slayer was built next to it in the 13th century.

The Once and Future Kings

Deep under the castle is a hall whose walls are hung with banners, armour and weapons. Amid great noise and merriment, the past kings of Poland hold an endless banquet. On New Year's Eve, Bolesław the Bold climbs the stairs to check on things in the castle. He is invisible to sinners but good men may glimpse him and his flashing sword. When Poland is in direst need, the kings will arm themselves and save the day. This legend was first recorded in the

19th century when many Poles clung to the hope that Poland might regain independence. The hill is riddled with caves of all shapes and sizes but in 1565 Zygmunt II the August ordered the cave entrances to be sealed. Smocza Jama (Dragon's Den, see p84) is the only one now open.

Alchemy and the Chicken's Foot

Zygmunt III Vasa (1566–1632) was a great patron of alchemy, whose laboratory was said to be in Kurza Stopka (Chicken's Foot) tower. The pope sent him a golden reliquary containing a saint's arm. Zygmunt set aside the arm, but performed experiments with the gold. The offended saint caused the melted gold to splash out of the window, leaving a discoloured streak down the tower. The king, disconcerted, left Wawel forever and moved to Warsaw.

One of his alchemists was Sendivogius (Michał Sędziwój, 1566–1636), who also served Emperor Rudolph II in Prague. An experiment in 1595 ended in an explosion and much of Wawel Castle burnt down. The greenish streak down the wall comes from rainwater running off the bronze roof.

The Wawel Chakra

Some say that, before the Slavs wandered into the Vistula valley, the sage Apollonius of Tyana (c. AD 3–97) hid a mystical stone on Wawel Hill. This stone is a chakra (energy focus point) of the earth, controlling the energy of all Europe. It is somewhere under the Chapel of St Gereon in the northern corner of the castle courtyard. Standing near the stone assists in 'aligning' one's own energy. Many Cracovians firmly believe that Krakow is a Hindu holy site, visited by pilgrims, including Nehru, India's first Prime Minister.

This idea started about 1932 when members of the Theosophical Society visited Wawel and declared the Chapel of St Gereon (rediscovered in 1916) to be a geyser of energy that radiated for thousands of miles. There are Indian members of Theosophy, but a quick survey indicates that few Hindus had heard of the Wawel Chakra before reading a Krakow guidebook. Nehru did visit Wawel, but there is no evidence that he knew of the chakra.

The legend is strongly disliked by the Museum and the Cathedral, who forbid certified guides even to mention it. The spot is easy to find: there are usually people meditating by the wall of the (closed) chapel. Superstitious Poles believe it necessary to lean against the wall for about ten minutes a week in order to benefit from the vital energy of the Chakra. There is even a stain on the wall where many people have tried their luck!

Opposite: the worst case of indigestion in Krakow's history!

Museums

Krakow has 43 museums, not counting private galleries or bars and cafés that display art. Whatever your taste, there's a good chance Krakow has a museum to suit. Ask at the Cultural Information Centre on ul. św. Jana about museums not on this list. Most museum information can be found at *www.krakow-info.com*

Czartoryski Museum bridge

Bunkier Sztuki (Art Bunker)

A bellicose concrete bunker interrupted by a bourgeois townhouse form a metaphor for post-modern art. The startling juxtaposition of old and new, begun in 1959 to designs by Różycki, salvaged elements of two older buildings. In the days of lock-step Socialist Realism, this was truly revolutionary art. One building was the Viennese-style Drobner Café whose ghost lives on in the very artistic coffee house. Krakow's foremost avant-garde gallery showcases active artists and ventures into multimedia and installations.
Pl. Szczepańska 3a (enter from Planty gardens). Tel: (012) 421 3840, 422 1052; fax: 422 8303. www.bunkier.com.pl. Open: Tue–Sun 11am–6pm (last admissions 5.30pm).

Muzeum Archeologiczne (Archaeological Museum)

This stately storehouse has one of the best collections of Slavic antiquities in Poland, including the Światowid of Zbrucz, the only major example of a pre-Christian stone idol anywhere in the Slavic world. The museum is very relaxed about visitors getting up close to such a famous artefact. Krakow's earliest history is shown by reconstructed cityscapes and artefacts excavated in the city. There is a small but well-presented collection of Egyptian mummies with high-tech analysis of what lies inside. A Tęczyński family palace on this site was converted into a monastery and then, in 1797, into a prison. The rose gardens offer abstract ceramic sculptures and a stunning view

Art for all tastes is on display

of Wawel. On Sundays entrance is free.
*ul. Poselska 3. Tel: (012) 422 7560.
Open: Mon–Wed, Fri 10am–2pm, Thur
2–6pm, Sun 10am–2pm.*

Muzeum Etnograficzne (Ethnographic Museum)
(*see pp100–01*)

Muzeum Historyczne Miasta Krakowa (City of Krakow Historical Museum)

This large museum boasts its own ghost,
the Black Lady, upstairs and its own
Devil in the cellars. The museum has
two entrances next to each other. That
on the right leads to the small space
that hosts some of the most interesting
exhibitions in town (such as the Szopki,
see pp60–1). The left-hand entrance
leads to the slightly musty but eclectic
permanent exhibits on the lives of
Cracovians through the ages, with a

The Old Synagogue is now a museum of Jewish
history and culture

Retired trams on display at the Museum of
Urban Technology

collection of burial urns representing their
deaths. This was the first city history
museum in Poland, opened in 1899.
*Rynek Główny 35. Tel: (012) 422 9922.
Open: Sun 9am–3pm, Wed 9am–3.30pm,
Thur 11am–6pm, Fri & Sat 9am–3.30pm.
Closed: Mon & Tue. Admission charge.*

Stara Synagoga (Old Synagogue)
This branch of the Historical Museum is
dedicated to the old Jewish Quarter in
Kazimierz (*see p102*).

Muzeum Inżynierii Miejskiej (Museum of Urban Technology)
(*see p101*)

Muzeum Katedralne (Cathedral Museum)
(*see pp83–4*)

Muzeum Narodowe (National Museum)

This shockingly serious-looking building is not communist-era, as you might suppose, but inter-war, one end of a line of monumental civic buildings. It houses a comprehensive collection of the established artists of 20th-century Poland and smaller displays of Polish decorative arts and military insignia. The insightful temporary exhibits are often thematic or focus on a single artist. *Al. 3 Maja 1. Tel: (012) 295 5500; fax: 633 9767. Open: Tue, Thur 10am–4pm, Wed, Fri, Sat 10am–7pm, Sun 10am–3.30pm. Closed: Mon.*

Centrum Sztuki i Techniki Japońskiej 'Manggha' (Manggha Centre of Japanese Art and Technology)

This undulating wave-like building, imitating the river below, was built in 1994 and paid for by Krakow's Oscar-winning film director, Andrzej Wajda. Its permanent collection includes Japanese and other Oriental art gathered by Feliks Jasieński (1861–1929), whose nickname was 'Manggha'. Visiting exhibitions bring Japan's best living artists to Krakow, and the centre hosts special events to increase awareness of Japanese culture (Children's Day, Tea

The National Museum

Ceremonies). Its teahouse has a view of Wawel across the river.
ul. Konopnickiej 26. Tel: (012) 267 2703, 267 3753. www.manggha.krakow.pl. Open: Tue–Sun 10am–6pm (last admissions 5.30pm). Closed: Mon & every third Sun.

Galeria w Sukiennicach (Cloth Hall Gallery)

Surprisingly, many visitors overlook this breathtaking exhibition of 19th-century and early 20th-century art. The huge canvases of historical paintings like Matejko's *Hold Pruski* (*Prussian Oath of Fealty*) and Siemiradzki's *Pochodnie Nerona* (*Nero's Torches*) are audacious in both size and detail. Stranger things lurk in Malczewski's obsessive symbolist self-portraits and the unhinged frenzy of Podkowiński's scandalous *Szał*. Do not leave without a look.
Rynek Główny 1/3 (entrance on outside of Sukiennice, opposite EMPiK). Tel: (012) 422 1166. Open: Tue, Fri & Sat 10am–7pm, Wed & Thur 10am–4pm, Sun 10am–3pm. Closed: Mon.

Muzeum Czartoryskich (Czartoryski Museum)

The communists made this a branch of the National Museum but it is the oldest public museum in Poland and one of the oldest in the world. Founded in buildings owned by the Czartoryski family near their palace in Puławy (in Russian Poland), it was moved to Paris to avoid tsarist confiscation and only in 1876 to Krakow, in liberal Habsburg Poland. The museum houses a small but important collection of Old Masters, including Leonardo da Vinci's famous

Czartoryski Museum

Lady with an Ermine (one of only three surviving oil portraits by him) and Rembrandt's *Landscape with the Good Samaritan*. Many artefacts and portraits depict the eventful history of the Czartoryskis. The well-chosen ancient artefacts include Egyptian, Greek and Roman art, but it is the less well-known Etruscan art that most impresses.
ul. św Jana 19 (entrance at ul. Pijarów 8). Tel: (012) 422 5566. Open: Tue, Thur 9am–3pm; Wed, Fri 11am–5pm, Sat–Sun 10am–3pm. Closed: every third Sun.

Muzeum Pamięci Narodowej 'Apteka pod Orłem' ('Pharmacy under the Sign of the Eagle' Museum of National Memory)

(*see pp110–11*)

Museum Uniwersytetu Jagiellońskiego Collegium Maius (Jagiellonian University Museum Collegium Maius)

(*see p68*)

Muzeum Zoologiczne, Filia w Collegium Iuridicum (Zoological Museum, Collegium Iuridicum Branch)

Deep in the cellars of the Art History department of the Jagiellonian University, this humble but charming museum displays the iridescent splendours of the insect kingdom.

The building itself is well worth a look around. Its appearance dates from the late-Gothic reconstruction (after a fire in 1455) of two buildings which were bought for the Faculty of Law in the 1400s.

ul. Grodzka 53. Tel: (012) 633 6377.
Open: Mon–Fri 10am–2pm,
Sun 11am–2pm.

Pałac Sztuki (Palace of Arts)

The finest Krakow building entirely in Art Nouveau style. Erected between 1898 and 1901, it represents itself as a temple of Apollo, patron of the Arts,

South American butterflies in the Zoological Museum

whose head hovers in a burst of light over the main door. The rich exterior portrays Faith, Hope and Love on one side, Doubt, Despair and Pain on the other. Busts of great 19th-century Polish painters rest in niches. It belongs to the Friends of the Fine Arts who choose a variety of media and subjects for the rotating exhibits (including painting, sculpture, photography, graphics and architectural designs). There is also an archive dedicated to Karol Estreicher Jr, an academic whose vision of the city influenced restoration of post-war Krakow.

Pl. Szczepański 4. Tel: (012) 422 6616. www.palac-sztuki.krakow. Open: daily 8.15am–6pm.

Zamek Królewski (Royal Castle)
(*see pp84–5*)

Wawel Hill is home to a whole complex of museums

Kazimierz

The long island between two branches of the Wisła (Vistula) river was home to two ancient settlements. Skałka (Cliff) was a pagan religious centre before the coming of Christianity. Downstream, near where the two branches rejoined, was the village of Bawół.

Jewish district, Kazimierz

In 1335, Kazimierz the Great named a new town on the island after himself, engulfing the older settlements. The western, upstream, end of the island was for religious orders. The middle section was laid out for burghers and trade. The king probably planned to build the new Academia Cracoviensis at the eastern end.

The town had its own defensive walls, main square and town hall. It was also graced with the Pons Regalis, the only bridge over this section of the Wisła. At its peak, Kazimierz boasted 5,000 inhabitants – Poles, Jews (Sephardi and Ashkenazi), Germans, Czechs, Walloons and Italians. It remained separate until 1791, when it became a district of Krakow, but only in 1880 was it physically joined to the city when the swampy and unhealthy Stara Wisła (Old Vistula) was filled in. Nowadays ul. Dietla runs above the old riverbed.

The Jewish District in Kazimierz

In 1494, fire destroyed part of the Jewish district in Krakow and the Jews were then blamed for starting the blaze. The King, Jan I Olbracht, set aside some land in Kazimierz (possibly where Kazimierz the Great had hoped to build the Academia Cracoviensis) and 'strongly encouraged' mass settlement of Jews on the island.

In 1553, this *kahal* (community) won the right to erect a wall to divide Jews from Gentiles, for security against unruly Catholic youth. As Jewish immigrants poured in and land became scarce, the ghetto was grudgingly expanded, for the last time in 1608. Its wall became a restriction, as town authorities allowed few Jews to settle elsewhere.

In 1782, Emperor Joseph II, distrusting the Jewish state-within-a-state, took away the powers of the *kahal* and encouraged Jews to assimilate. The ghetto walls were torn down in 1822. Soon the trickle of Jews out of Kazimierz became a steady flow.

In 1935, Majer Bałaban wrote of the lost vibrancy of the ghetto: 'Today, Jews live throughout Krakow and all of its suburbs... [but] in the "Jewish City" only the poor and the ultra-conservative' – those without money or inclination to renovate their dilapidated tenements. The district remained little changed until the 1990s when renewed interest in Krakow's Jewish heritage brought new cafés, hotels and shops.

Cmentarz Żydowski 'Nowy' ('New' Jewish Cemetery)

Although improved considerably from its nadir in the 1980s, the New Jewish Cemetery seems shockingly overgrown and uncared-for compared to the immaculately groomed Catholic cemeteries. Apart from the strangling vegetation, youngsters from the high school opposite leave graffiti and vodka bottles in darker corners of the graveyard.

The New Cemetery – opened in 1800, when Remuh cemetery was closed – was built outside the walls of Kazimierz and the ghetto. This is now Krakow's only active Jewish cemetery: you will find recent graves of the rapidly-dwindling community to the right of the entrance. In two places monuments are assembled from the broken tombstones of Krakow's other Jewish cemeteries, now gone. The Nazis used Jewish tombstones to pave the roads in the Płaszów concentration camp. What could be recovered was brought here.

Most visitors reach the cemetery by passing under the railway at the narrow underpass on ul. Miodowe. Visitors are expected to cover their heads. If you have no head-covering, you can hire a small paper hat from the porter.
ul. Miodowej 55. Open: Sun–Fri sunrise to sunset. Trams: 3, 9, 13, 24.

Kościół Bożego Ciała (Corpus Christi Church)

Work started in 1340 on this magnificent Gothic church, planned by Kazimierz the Great to be the main sanctuary of his new town. Rarely visited by tourists, its spacious walled churchyard is quiet and calm. Burials here ceased in 1857. Under a roof by the main gate, Jesus prays in the Garden of Gethsemane while his disciples sleep. An angel offers a chalice to hearten him for his coming suffering. The sculptures are 16th-century.

The octagonal belfry tower, topped by a Baroque crown, is reminiscent of the Mariacki church. Likewise, Bożego Ciała was planned with two towers but the second was never built. The stone arches of the nave and aisles have been laid bare, their simplicity contrasting with the ornate Baroque altars and the flamboyant pulpit shaped like a ship held aloft by dolphins and mermaids, with angels flitting about the sail.
ul. Bożego Ciała 26. Trams: 6, 8, 10.

Kościół św. Katarzyny (St Catherine's Church)

A tall, graceful and airy Gothic church raised by Kazimierz the Great

The wheel of Death at Kościół św. Katarzyny – 'Death has reigned since Adam'

for the Austin Friars that he settled here in the 1360s. Over the entrance from ul. Skałeczna hangs an immense 17th- or 18th-century Wheel of Death (Catherine's symbol is the wheel she was tortured on). Among the figures crowding this complex allegory are the three Fates, measuring lives in a grotto, and Adam and Eve clutching a single apple. The central eight-spoked wheel contains skulls wearing the headgear of kings, princes, bishops and burghers. The cheery message to the worshippers below is 'Whatever your fortune, it will always end with death'. The corridors leading from the entrance on ul. Augustiańska are covered in 15th-century frescoes, rich in allegory and scenes from the lives of saints.
ul. Augustiańska 7. Trams: 6, 8, 10.

Kościół św. Michała i klasztor Paulinów 'Na Skałce' (St Michael's Church and the Pauline Fathers' Monastery 'on the Rock')

The first religious centre on Skałka (Cliff) was pre-Christian. On the site

A funerary chapel outside Kościół Bożego Ciała

was built an 11th-century Romanesque rotunda dedicated to St Michael, who fights the devil in the form of a dragon. This was, in turn, replaced by a Gothic church funded by Kazimierz the Great when Skałka was engulfed by his new town. Even that was torn down in 1733 to make way for a Baroque edifice.

The church is venerated as the site of the martyrdom of St Stanisław (Stanislaus) of Szczepanowo, Patron Saint of Poland. In one version of the story, Bishop Stanisław was executed in 1079 for supporting a revolt. The more saintly version claims that Stanisław reproached Bolesław the Bold for his immoral behaviour; the king was so enraged that he rushed down to Skałka to kill the saint himself. Among relics are the wooden beam on which the saint's body was hacked to pieces and a piece of wall, spattered with blood. The saint's body now rests in a silver casket on the altar of the Cathedral.

Below the church is the Krypta Zasłużonych (Crypt of the Worthy). Among those buried here are artists like Wyspiański and Malczewski, writers like Kraszewski, the composer Szymanowski and the medieval chronicler, Długosz.
ul. Skałeczna 1.

Muzeum Etnograficzne (Ethnographic Museum)

A permanent collection of Polish folk art: on the ground floor are reconstructions of 19th-century vernacular buildings, including a flax mill. Upstairs are regional costumes, Easter eggs, Nativity scenes, farm implements and musical instruments, among other things.

The building was Kazimierz's town hall, built after 1335 when the town was founded and completed by 1369 when its bells were installed. The building with a single tower overlooking a market square is typical of Central European town halls. At the end of the 19th century, Kazimierz was demoted to a district of Krakow and no longer needed a town hall. The museum was set up here after the Second World War.
Pl. Wolnica 1. Tel: (012) 430 5563. Open: Mon 10am–6pm, Wed–Fri 10am–3pm, Sat–Sun 10am–2pm

Muzeum Inżynierii Miejskiej (Museum of Urban Technology)

One of Krakow's newest museums, this focuses on public transport in

Inside Remuh Synagogue, Krakow's most active synagogue

Krakow but also features factories and construction. Old trams and buses are housed in an attractive tramshed. A trip here can be combined with go-karting in another tram depot across the street.
ul. św. Wawrzyńca 15. Tel: (012) 421 1242. Open: Tue–Sun 10am–4pm. Trams: 3, 9, 13, 24.

Remuh Synagogue and Cemetery

Krakow's only active Orthodox synagogue was founded by Israel ben Josef Isserles in 1553 for his son, the prodigious Rabbi Moses Isserles whose initials in Hebrew spell his popular name 'Remuh'. When the first synagogue burnt down, he received permission from Zygmunt II the August in 1556 to build a new one.

The gateway on ul. Szeroka still reads 'new synagogue, dedicated to the memory of Rabbi Remuh'. It is the smallest synagogue in Kazimierz but one of the most beautiful. The *bimah* (pulpit for reading the Torah) is reconstructed, but some furnishings were saved, including the Renaissance cupboard in the Jerusalem-facing wall that contains the Torah.

Remarkably, the cemetery next to it survived, partly because the Nazis failed to understand its significance and instead levelled newer and better-kept Jewish cemeteries. Writing in the 1930s, Majer Bałaban lamented that 'most of the monuments are destroyed, fallen to earth or lean brokenly against the bases of those still standing ... very few stones are left and the epitaphs can be read on only a few headstones'. During recent renovation it turned out that many tombstones that Bałaban saw had, in fact, been buried intentionally, to save them from some previous danger. The grave of Remuh is set apart by a low fence and usually covered with small stones and pieces of paper, remnants of prayers said at his grave. The impressive cemetery wall is lined with fragments of gravestones found by archaeologists.

Visitors are expected to pay a small entrance fee and cover their heads. If you have no head-covering, you can hire a small paper hat from the porter. *ul. Szeroka 40. Open: Mon–Fri 9am–4pm. Trams: 3, 9, 13, 24.*

Stara Synagoga (Old Synagogue)

No longer an active house of worship, this is a branch of the Historical

Interior of Tempel Synagogue

Museum showing everyday life in the Jewish ghetto before the Holocaust. Most of the original furnishings were destroyed by the Nazis. The iron *bimah* is a reconstruction of the 16th-century original.

Although its exact date is unknown, Stara Synagoga is probably the oldest still standing in Poland. A synagogue may have stood here before the mass arrival of Jews from Krakow proper from 1494. Fire destroyed the Gothic synagogue in 1556, and a new one was built by the Italian architect, Matthew Gucci. He incorporated some Renaissance ideas, but retained a lot of Gothic features like the two-nave main hall. *ul. Szeroka 24. Tel: (012) 422 0962. Open: Mon 10am–2pm, Tue–Sun 10am–5pm. Trams: 3, 9, 13, 24.*

Synagoga Izaaka (Isaac's Synagogue)

This was the most ostentatious of Krakow's synagogues and it remains the largest. The rich merchant Izaak Jakubowicz received the king's permission to build the synagogue in 1638, but at first it stood empty because the priests of Kościół św. Wawrzyniec (St Lawrence's Church, now gone) protested they could not carry communion wafers within sight of a synagogue.

Izaaka was devastated by the Nazis. Several layers of frescoes from the 17th and 18th centuries have since been restored in patches around the main hall. The ceiling and women's gallery are decorated with Baroque stucco. Since conservation work was completed in 1995, the synagogue has acted as a

Unique stained glass at Tempel Synagogue

Tempel was built during 1860–62, symbolically outside the old ghetto, by a group of Jews who had largely assimilated into Polish culture. Controversially it featured stained-glass windows with dedications in Polish, organ music and choral singing, which drove Orthodox Jews to fury. Much of the rich painted plasterwork draws its inspiration from the *Sefardi* (Iberian Jewish) tradition, fusing pseudo-Moorish with neo-Renaissance.

Visitors are expected to pay a small entrance fee and cover their heads. If you have no head-covering, you can hire a small paper hat from the porter. *ul. Miodowa 24. Trams: 19, 22.*

private gallery. The cost of admission includes two short documentary films, on a video loop, about pre-war Kazimierz and the Podgórze Ghetto. *ul. Jakuba 25. Trams: 3, 9, 13, 24.*

Synagoga Tempel (Tempel Synagogue)

Krakow's only active Reformed synagogue is not very active except when Remuh is being renovated. Since the last cantor died in 1985, services occur only often enough to keep up appearances.

RABBI MOSES ISSERLES

'From Moses to Moses there has been no-one like Moses' his tombstone declares. Moses Isserles (c.1520–72) was valued by many Jews as second only to Moses the prophet. Popularly known by his acronym 'Remuh', he became chief rabbi of Krakow about 1547, and then rector of the *yeshiva* (Talmud school) and head of the *kahal* (Jewish community)

Remuh was a commentator on many texts and burning issues. His writings sought to unify philosophy and Jewish mysticism. He also brought together the traditions of different Jewish communities in Krakow, including Ashkenazim (literally 'German' – Yiddish-speaking, from Central and Eastern Europe) and Sefardim (speaking a form of medieval Spanish, from Southern Europe or Muslim countries). He was instrumental in creating the unique culture of Krakow's Jews.

Walk: Jewish Kazimierz

There were other Jewish districts (*notably Podgórze, see p108*) but the exodus of richer Jews from the narrow streets of eastern Kazimierz preserved an older and more picturesque look. The absence of the original Jewish inhabitants has been balanced out by a growing artistic community.

Allow 1¹/₂ hours.

Start at the corner of ul. Bożego Ciała and ul. Meiselsa.

1 Into the Ghetto

From 1608 until 1822, tall walls ran along ul. Bożego Ciała, separating the worlds of Jew and Gentile. Today the ghetto is open to all, but the community

has vanished as completely as their walls. As you wander down ul. Meiselsa (named after a rabbi who supported Polish independence), look through the gate to your right into one of the most

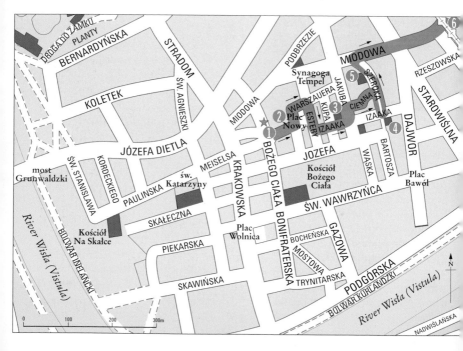

picturesque alleys in Kazimierz. Just beyond, at the corner of the square, is an old prayer-house, now a Jewish Cultural Centre. There is not much Jewish culture in Krakow today; the centre is mostly for the benefit of Poles who are curious about their former neighbours.
Continue into the square.

2 Plac Nowy/Plac Żydowski (New Square/Jewish Square)

Although it is shown as Plac Nowy (New Square) on all city maps, asking for directions by that name will get you blank looks from the locals. It is universally known as Plac Żydowski (Jewish Square). On Sunday mornings there is a busy clothing bazaar. Other days, a more sedate vegetable market occupies the stalls. On warm summer nights, in spite of the law against drinking on the street, cafés and bars

spill out into the square to form one giant beer garden. The pensioners who live in the rent-controlled housing around the square have been known to throw potatoes at unusually loud revellers. Alchemia is a good spot to sample the spirits, or pop into Les Couleurs Café for a slice of quiche and an espresso.
Loop clockwise around the square to the mouth of ul. Izaaka.

3 Isaac's Synagogue

At the corner of ul. Izaaka you pass a small café named Singer (pronounced 'zing-ger') after the Singer sewing machines that serve as tables. In the mid-1990s it was one of the first *knajpe* to draw nightlife down into Kazimierz again. It has cultivated an artistic gloom ever since and remains a mainstay. In front of you rises the Baroque Isaac's

A Jewish café on ul. Szeroka

Synagogue (*see pp102–03*), painstakingly renovated to recapture some of its earlier charm. On Friday evenings at sundown, the smaller prayer-house next door hosts a Jewish youth group. Continue to the small square at the start of ul. Ciemna. Eden Hotel on the left has the only *mikveh* (Jewish ritual bath) in use in Krakow and can serve kosher meals if you order in advance.

Follow ul. Ciemna, which meanders a little to the right and left before emptying into ul. Szeroka.

4 Old Synagogue

At ul. Szeroka (Wide Street) you reach the easternmost edge of medieval Kazimierz and the heart of the ghetto. In front of you, closing off the square is Stara Synagoga (Old Synagogue), the oldest synagogue still standing in Krakow, now a museum of Jewish history (*see p102*). In front of it are two monuments: one to Kościuszko, who on this spot raised Jewish support for his uprising in 1794, the other to Poles

The cemetery walls are partially made of broken tombstones

Izaac's Synagogue

executed here in 1943 (all Jews had been removed from Krakow earlier that year). Past the synagogue is a reconstructed fragment of city wall. Beyond this point, Kazimierz's island was too swampy for stonework. The bank close to the Old Synagogue is sometimes mistakenly identified as the Synagoga Na Górce (Upstairs Synagogue) that once stood here. A renowned bastion of kabala mysticism, it was torn apart by treasure seekers looking for alchemists' gold after the war.

Wander down to the other end of this short and wide street.

5 Remuh Synagogue

On the right-hand side, behind an iron gate, is the rather drab Popper's Synagogue, now stripped of all decoration and converted into an art centre. On the left-hand side of the street is Remuh Synagogue, tiny in size but a giant in Jewish culture (*see pp101–02*). It serves a small, elderly congregation, augmented on the Sabbath and holidays by pilgrims from all over the world. The cemetery behind it contains many illustrious forefathers but the most famous is Rabbi Moses Isserles (*see p103*). The grassy plot at the centre of the street was once the Jewish cemetery. Later, a legend arose that it marked the spot where Sabbath-breakers were swallowed up into the earth. A stone stands in memory of the many lives lost in the Holocaust. The tall building at the end of the street is the Landau Palace, once home to one of the richest families in the Oppidum. The low building to the right was the *mikveh* (Jewish ritual bath

house); you can see some original columns in the dining rooms of the ground-floor restaurant.

Pass between the Landau Palace and the Mikveh to ul. Miodowa and cross (carefully) ul. Starowiślna. Walk carefully through the narrow underpass (cars drive in both directions and cannot see pedestrians on the opposite side).

6 New Cemetery

Enter through the gate to your right. A ghostly reminder of Krakow's lost Jewish community, the New Cemetery slumbers in magnificent decay (*see p99*). The narrow alleys are broken and overgrown. The three large monuments were built from tombstones of other cemeteries that did not survive. Please remember to cover your head.

The 'New' Jewish Cemetery is already over 200 years old

Podgórze and Płaszów

Although Podgórze officially became part of Krakow only in 1915, the district on the far side of the river has ancient ties with the city.

An old doorway in Podgórze

Podgórze became part of the Habsburg dominion in the First Partition of Poland (1772). In order to compete with Krakow proper, Emperor Joseph II in 1784 declared the sleepy collection of hamlets a 'royal city' with special privileges and tax breaks. The building of factories was encouraged and craftsmen were offered cash incentives to come and settle. With Poland's economy in a tailspin, many accepted and Podgórze grew quickly.

However, in 1795, the Third Partition brought Krakow into the Habsburg fold, making the rivalry moot. When the Free City of Krakow (*see p114*) was created in 1815, Podgórze remained in Habsburg hands. Once again, an international border divided Krakow and Podgórze, until Krakow rejoined the Habsburg portfolio in 1846. Finally, in the dying days of the Austro-Hungarian Empire, Podgórze was incorporated into Krakow.

In 1941, Nazi forces created the Krakow Ghetto in a few blocks of a Jewish neighbourhood around Plac Zgody (Concord Square – now renamed Plac Bohaterów Getta – Square of the Heroes of the Ghetto). (*See pp109, 110–11.*)

Cmentarz Podgórski

Unusually, Podgórze cemetery does not have separate sections for Protestants and Roman Catholics. It was probably founded shortly after the village was given city status in 1784 and the most illustrious individual to rest in this hallowed ground is Edward Dembowski (1822–46), a hero of one of Poland's many failed uprisings. He was gunned down in Podgórze when he and a crowd of independence-minded Poles brandishing religious icons and weapons approached a nervous Austrian garrison. The soldiers did not ask which he intended to use before opening fire.

Nearby, you can see the sculpture of God the Father on his column. It originally stood at the Wielicka Gate that marked the border of Podgórze. After the gate was torn down, the column was moved at least three times but it returned to its current position in honour of ten Poles shot by the Nazis in 1943 in retaliation for the assassination of an informant.

Fabryka Telpod (Schindler's Factory)

The Rekord Factory was built in 1938 to produce enamelled pots and pans. During the Second World War, profiteer Oscar Schindler (1908–74) took over the factory and produced bomb parts and mess kits for Nazi soldiers. Jews in the nearby Ghetto paid to have their names entered on Schindler's list of indispensable employees, thereby saving themselves from deportation. Even though the factory could be run with

50 employees, Schindler had 1,200 names on his list. The factory was confiscated after the war. There are no official tours, but for a small tip guards are usually willing to show visitors around the building, much of which still looks as it did during the war.
ul. Lipowa 4. Tel: (012) 257 1011.

Ghetto Walls

In two places you can still see fragments of the wall of the Nazi Ghetto (1941–3). One is just round the corner from Podgórze cemetery, behind the school at ul. Limanowskiego 62. The other is between Nos. 25 and 29 on ul. Lwowska. The Ghetto wall was originally 3m (10ft) tall and had only four gates. It was built on orders from Governor Otto Wächter (1901–49). According to the Italian novelist Curzio Malaparte, Wächter's wife praised the wall as 'in an oriental style with beautiful arches and crenellation. Cracovian Jews really don't have anything to complain about. A real elegant wall in Hebrew taste.' Jews who tried to go outside the Ghetto walls without permission were shot.

Kopiec Kraka (Krak's Mound)

Legend claims this as the burial mound of King Krak, founder of Krakow (*see p90*). It is also known as Rękawka, supposedly because Krak's mourning subjects carried sand in their sleeves (*rękawki*) to help build it.

An archaeological dig in 1934–7 did not uncover a royal burial, but it did turn up some surprises. Below the surface was the stump of an oak tree that had lived over 300 years on the top of the mound before being cut, probably about the time

A surviving fragment of the Ghetto walls on ul. Lwowska

that Christianity was adopted in Krakow. Even further into the mound was an Avar ornament, suggesting that the mound was raised in about the 7th century.

The upper layers of the mound were sprinkled with coins from the 13th to the 19th centuries. They are a reminder of the ancient Cracovian festival, also called Rękawka, when the nobility of the town would scatter riches on Easter Tuesday. Today, Rękawka is celebrated with a funfair in April, lots of sweets and popcorn, and a camp of 9th-century Slavic warriors who put on sword fights and archery demonstrations.

Kościół św. Benedykta (St Benedict's Church)

An early Romanesque church already stood on this spot at the turn of the 11th century, probably part of the manor buildings of a local chieftain. Rebuilt several times, its Baroque shape was

finalised in 1598. It is especially beautiful in spring when the fruit trees are in flower.

Legend tells of a beautiful but greedy princess cursed to live under the altar. She has been known to approach young men with sacks of gold in an effort to free herself from the centuries of captivity. If the young man spends all the money on himself within a set period of time, the princess will be set free. However, if he spends a single *grosz* on anyone else, he is doomed to be decapitated by the angry princess. *The easiest way to reach the church is by ul. Rękawka.*

Muzeum Pamięci Narodowej 'Apteka pod Orłem' ('Pharmacy Under the Sign of the Eagle' Museum of National Memory)

When the Ghetto was created in 1941, Tadeusz Pankiewicz (1908–93) found

Climb Kopiec Kraka for a view of the city

Schindler's factory has hardly changed since the Second World War

that his pharmacy was inside the walls. Other Gentiles escaped elsewhere as Jews poured in, but Pankiewicz remained and kept his shop open. He was an invaluable source of medicine and contact with the outside world for the next two years. In 1982 the pharmacy was converted into a museum dedicated to the Ghetto.
Plac Bohaterów Getta 18. Tel: (012) 422 8566. Open: Mon–Fri 10am–4pm, Sat 10am–2pm. Closed: Sun.

Park Bednarskiego
This graceful little park is named after Wojciech Bednarski (1841–1914), who campaigned to have the old quarry filled in and planted. The limestone cliffs give the impression of wild terrain and the views over Krakow are spectacular. According to legend, Pan Twardowski (*see p63*) was supposed to have taught black magic to his students in caves in these rocks.
Entrance from ul. Parkowa.

THE NAZI GHETTO AND *SCHINDLER'S LIST*

The Jewish Ghetto was created in Podgórze in March 1941. The Nazis herded the remaining 20,000 Jews from the Krakow area into a mere 329 buildings (*see p108*). The Ghetto was liquidated on 13–14 March 1943. Thousands of Jews were shot on the spot; the rest were sent to concentration camps, which most of them did not survive.

Oscar Schindler ran a factory in Podgórze (*see pp108–09*) during the war. The true story of Schindler's famous list of 'essential' employees was the basis for Thomas Keneally's novel *Schindler's Ark*, which won the 1983 Booker Prize. In 1993, Steven Spielberg made a film based on the book and won seven Oscars, bringing Schindler's story to the attention of cinema-goers worldwide.

However, in spite of the terrible fame of the Ghetto, few visitors to Krakow can point it out on the map and even fewer bother to seek it out. Unlike the picturesque Jewish Quarter of Kazimierz where Spielberg's film was shot, the real site of the Nazi Ghetto across the river has remained a working-class neighbourhood with only one subdued museum to the horrors it has witnessed (*see pp110–11*).

Walk: Podgórze, the Austrian Rival

Once a serious rival to the main city, Podgórze is now a rather unassuming district of Krakow. Although its tourist attractions are less spectacular than those of Wawel or Rynek Główny, they possess their own quiet charm.
Allow 1¹/₂ hours.

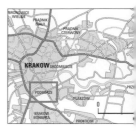

The terrain around Podgórze is very hilly and unpaved in places. Remember to wear sensible shoes. Start the walk at Rynek Podgórski. The easiest way to get there from the city centre is by tram.

1 Rynek Podgórski
Nearly triangular, Rynek Podgórski is closed by Kościół św. Józefa. Founded

in 1832, it was rebuilt in 1909 – to plans by Jan Sas-Zubrzycki (1860–1935) – to look more like Kościół Mariacki on Krakow's Rynek Główny. The large building on your left was the town hall of Podgórze until 1915.
Walk past the church and up the hill, following ul. Rękawka until nearly to the end.

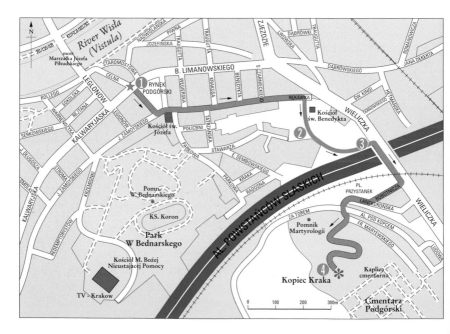

2 St Benedict's Hill

As you climb the hill, you pass the place where the city gallows stood in the Middle Ages, lending this area the name Na Zbóju (For Killing). At the beginning of the 20th century, the area was gentrified with upmarket, two-storey houses, many of whose inhabitants were Jewish. The house at No. 30 was a Jewish school. Looking down ul. Węgierska to the left, you can glimpse a Jewish prayer-house at No. 5.

At the top of the hill, continue into the field where the road stops. To the left is the little church of St Benedict's (*see p110*). From the church come the popular names of the hill itself and the tower known as St Benedict's Fort. The huge brick polygon is the survivor of a pair built in 1852 as Maximilian's Bastions. The rest of the fortifications were dismantled at the turn of the 20th century.

Beyond the fort, there is a footpath leading downhill to the left.

3 Cmentarz Podgórski

Although it is difficult to see from the path, there is a small surviving fragment of the Nazi Ghetto wall to your left. (Do not stray too far from the path. There are some very steep drops.) Continue along the wall of the old Podgórze cemetery (*see p108*), situated outside the town walls as stipulated by Habsburg law. Take a minute to wander through its melancholic aisles.

Cross over the busy Al. Powstańców, walk past the kiosks and into the pedestrian tunnel leading under the railway tracks. Turn right on

ul. Robotnicza and start climbing uphill again. Robotnicza merges into Lanckorońska. Bear left and follow the steps up the hill until it turns into a dirt track.

4 Kopiec Kraka

At the top of the hill is the hoary earthwork known as Krak's Mound (*see pp109–10*). From its summit, you have a spectacular view of Krakow and its environs. Below you is the Liban stone quarry, with pieces of the film-set for *Schindler's List* still visible at its swampy bottom. The real Płaszów Forced Labour Camp was not far away. To visit the camp's rubble and scattered ruins, just continue along the path away from the city centre past the new cemetery.

Kościół św. Benedykta

The Habsburg Empire and the Free City

The last king of Poland, Stanisław August Poniatowski (1732–98) was elected to the throne in 1764 as a puppet of the Russian Empire. A man of Enlightenment ideals, he mistakenly believed that Catherine the Great would tolerate the reforms, including Europe's first constitution, that he tried to introduce in Poland. Rather than allow such radical politics on their doorsteps, Russia, Prussia and the Habsburgs carved up and annexed the Commonwealth Kingdom of Poland and Lithuania. Poniatowski abdicated in 1795 and Poland ceased to exist.

Krakow found itself in a new province, the 'Kingdom of Galicia and Lodomeria' – territory that now belongs to southern Poland and western Ukraine – part of the Habsburg dynasty's mismatched portfolio of titles and real estate. Although its official language became German shortly after Poland's partition, the Habsburg Empire also embraced Magyars, Czechs, Slovaks, Croats, Serbs, Slovenes, Italians, Romanians, Poles and Ruthenians. Already an empire in decline, the Habsburgs clung to their position by a combination of political marriages and carefully playing off enemies. Their loyal servants were the legions of bureaucrats whose powers reached into the most minute details of everyday life.

As the Napoleonic wars swept Europe, the stateless Poles became pawns in the game. In 1807 Napoleon created the Grand Duchy of Warsaw from the Polish-speaking lands of conquered Prussia. In 1809, the duchy took over Krakow and held it until Waterloo in 1815.

At the Congress of Vienna, Russia re-acquired most of the Grand Duchy but the Habsburgs still claimed Krakow. With no agreement who would have it, the 'Free, Independent and Strictly Neutral City of Krakow' was invented. Krakow more or less governed itself as a separate country, monitored by three Residents who represented the conquering powers. The little state became famous for legal trade and smuggling. However, in 1846 student radicals attempted to revive a Polish

state in one of the least competent uprisings in Poland's long history of failed revolts. Krakow was returned to Habsburg control.

In 1867, Franz Joseph I found it expedient to reshuffle his collection of titles into the Dual Monarchy of Austria-Hungary. The Magyar peoples were seduced away from open revolt by being allowed to run their kingdom of Hungary. Other peoples of the empire soon manoeuvred for similar status. In exchange for unswerving loyalty to the Emperor himself, the Poles in 1871 got their own Minister for Galicia, who could circumvent the bureaucrats.

The period from 1871 is fondly remembered in Krakow as 'the Galician Autonomy' – the city and the Polish-speaking nobility prospered; Polish became the language of schools and universities; Polish poetry, theatre and visual arts flourished. Emperor Franz Joseph remained a popular but distant figurehead in Vienna, a jovial granddad whose portrait hung on the wall but whose decrees were largely ignored. In 1918, as the Habsburg Empire lay in ruins, Krakow was reunited with the partitioned territories of the other two occupying powers and Poland was reborn.

Krakow's churches were part of the 'Free, Independent and Strictly Neutral City of Krakow'

Salwator and Zwierzyniec

Salwator is the perfect place to take a slow, afternoon stroll on an early summer day (*see p120*). This turn-of-the-century district was lovingly designed with shaded walkways and integrated parks.

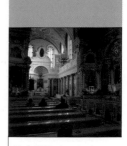

Kościół Norbertanek

Although it lies 2km (1¼ miles) west of the city centre, Zwierzyniec is one of the oldest districts in Krakow. In the 9th century, it had a palisade fortress where the Premonstratensian Convent now stands, and signs of pagan sanctuaries have been found at several points further up Blessed Bronisława's Hill. Guarding the western approach from the Żabi kruk swamp, Zwierzyniec was conquered and plundered by nearly every army that attacked Krakow.

In 1909, Zwierzyniec became part of Krakow. Influenced by the Garden City concept of Sir Ebenezer Howard, a new urban plan was developed for the residential area of Salwator, up the hill from the medieval church of the Holy Saviour. The new estates formed an organic whole of graceful villas and winding, tree-lined roads.

Salwator quickly gained a reputation as an artists' district and there are still many workshops and *ateliers* along the Rudawa river. Sculptor Stanisław Szukalski (1895–1987) led a group of students to revolt from the conservative Academy of Fine Arts in the 1930s to form Szczep Rogaty Serc (Tribe of the Horned Heart). Their hot-headed plans to found an alternative artists' colony in Salwator called Duchtynia (Soul-Shrine) were cooled by the impending threat of war.

Kopiec Kościuszki

General Tadeusz Andrzej Bonawentura Kościuszko (1746–1817) died a lonely exile in Switzerland. Under the relatively liberal government of the Free City of Krakow, a plan was laid to raise a monument to the Polish national hero. In 1820, inspired by the prehistoric mounds to Krak and Wanda, the citizens began work on the monument. Even the officers of the occupying Austrian garrison pitched in. Earth was brought to the mound from each of Kościuszko's Polish battlefields.

As the mound began to take shape, a mysterious ghost in a burial shroud and carrying a flaming torch haunted the site by night. At first the workers ran away but one army officer grew suspicious. He and two of his men captured the 'ghost' at bayonet-point, revealing him to be a local innkeeper. Work on the mound had taken away his customers and he was just trying to scare up a little business.

The mound was completed in 1823, but in 1846 Krakow was back in the Habsburg Empire. The new fortifications that encircled Krakow in 1854 made use of the Kościuszko Mound. Not only was it a perfect vantage point but the brick walls around its base were a highly visible symbol of who was in control.

On 4 July 1926, Eric P Kelley, a visiting American lecturer at the Jagiellonian University (*see p68*), lowered a box of earth taken from each of Kościuszko's American battlefields into the Kościuszko Mound. In 2002, the city authorities proudly unveiled a completely renovated mound, now equipped with a steel skeleton and complex drainage system, ensuring that the mound would last for generations to come.

At the end of ul. Waszyngtona. Bus: 100.

Kościół św. Małgorzaty (St Margaret's Church)

Local legend claims that this octagonal wooden church stands on the site of an ancient pagan shrine to the god Poświst, and was converted to Christian use by missionaries from Moravia.

The current church was built during 1680–90 when an earlier one burnt down. It was in the early 20th century when it picked up the nickname 'Gontyna' from a Romantic but mistaken reconstruction of the word for a Slavic temple (*continas* in Latin) from *gonty* (wooden shingles). When the streets of Salwator were named in 1911, the street just above St Margaret's was dubbed ul. Gontyna. Like the dedications of other churches on the sites of pagan shrines, St Margaret is often portrayed as a dragon-slayer.

ul. bł. Bronisławy.

Kopiec Kościuszki overlooks Zwierzyniec

Kościół i klasztor Norbertanek (The Premonstratensian Nuns' Church and Cloister)

Founded in the second half of the 12th century, the convent complex guards the main road from the west. Although fortified, it was overrun and pillaged by nearly every invader from the Tartars to the Swedes. Each destruction was followed by rebuilding, leaving this church rich in the architectural styles of eight centuries.

It is said that when the Tartars first destroyed the convent in 1241, they threw the church bell into the Wisła. Every year, on Midsummer Night (Feast of St John the Baptist), the bell rises to the surface of the river, rings once and then sinks back down.
ul. Kościuszki.

Kościół Najświętszego Salwatora (Church of the Most Holy Saviour)

One of the most ancient churches in the Krakow area, its exact date is a matter of controversy. Some scholars believe it was built before Poland's conversion to Roman Catholicism in 966 and belongs to a time when Krakow was a satellite of the Great Moravian Empire, which practised eastern-rite Christianity. Others prefer a date after Prince Mieszko's conversion and the establishment of a western-rite bishopric in Krakow.

One popular legend claims that Piotr Włostowic (*d.* 1153), steward of Prince Władysław II the Exile, funded its

---

THE *LAJKONIK*

On the first Thursday after Corpus Christi, the *Lajkonik* procession wends its way through the streets from the Premonstratensian Convent to Rynek Główny. A man wearing a bushy black beard and a tall conical hat adorned with Oriental motifs dances a hobby-horse through the crowds, surrounded by 30 or so brightly-garbed attendants. The man-horse carries a mace with which he gently taps children for good luck. When the exhausted dancer finally reaches the Rynek hours later, he is warmly greeted by the city authorities with a goblet of wine.

The story is that the tradition reaches back to the Tartars' third attack on Krakow, in 1281. A group of brave raftsmen made a raid on the tent of the khan. The Tartars were so surprised that they fled, leaving the raftsmen to parade into town riding the khan's best horse and wearing his finest silks.

Salwator is just a tram ride away

construction. Włostowic had slandered Władysław's first wife, Agnieszka. In revenge, she convinced the prince that Włostowic was planning a revolt, and he ordered Włostowic's tongue cut out and eyes put out. The innocent Włostowic appealed to the bishop of Krakow, who told him that if he founded seven churches and three monasteries, God would grant him his eyes and tongue back. Proud Włostowic overdid his penance and founded 70 churches and 30 monasteries, but did not get the promised reward. When he complained, the bishop pointed out that he had not followed his instructions exactly. Włostowic went out and founded exactly seven more churches and three more monasteries, at which he was miraculously healed.

Kościół Najświętszego Salwatora, a holy site for countless centuries

Walk: Salwator

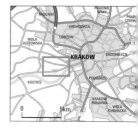

The best time of year to walk around Salwator is late spring or early summer when the flowers are in bloom. If you go on a Sunday morning about 10am, the churches will be open.

Allow 2 hours.

Start the walk at Kopiec Kościuszki. You can reach it easily by taking a No. 100 bus all the way to the terminus.

1 Kopiec Kościuszki (Kościuszko Mound)

Entering next to the Chapel of the Blessed Bronisława, take the time to walk to the top of the mound for the spectacular view of Krakow. There are no guard rails, which may leave visitors with vertigo a bit uneasy.

Follow the path back down to Al. Jerzego

Waszyngtona, the tree-lined road that runs towards the city centre.

2 Cmentarz Salwatorski and ul. Gontyna

The quiet little Salwator Cemetery was founded in 1865 when the old cemetery at Najświętszego Salwatora was closed because of overcrowding. Many of those

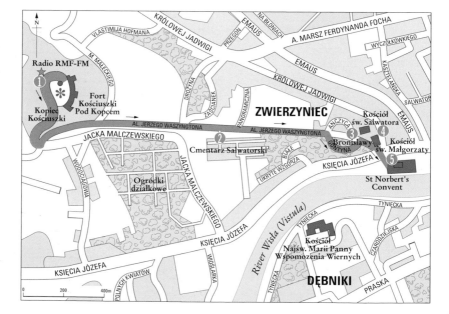

buried here belonged to the artistic community that congregated in this area in the early 20th century. Continue along Al. Jerzego Waszyngtona until you come to ul. Gontyna. Turn right for this charming assembly of villas inspired by Art Nouveau and built on the site of redundant military installations.

ul. Gontyna swings back to meet ul. św Bronisławy. Cross the road to Kościół Najświętszego Salwatora.

3 Kościół Najświętszego Salwatora (Church of the Most Holy Saviour)

If the church gate is open, take time to explore the slightly dilapidated cemetery. The oldest graves are from the 17th century but the cemetery was in use for centuries before that. The church is usually open only for mass and weddings so take the opportunity if you get it.

Cross back over the street and walk just a little downhill to the next church.

4 Kościół św. Małgorzaty (St Margaret's Church)

Generally, the gate is open only when a mass is being held. Perhaps they are trying to keep the pagans from taking back their shrine. In the 1940s, a tiny group of neo-pagans called Święte Koło Czcicieli Światowida (Sacred Circle of Światowid Worshippers) declared St Margaret's to be a temple of their religion but, though their publications used photographs of this odd edifice, they never took control of it.

Continue down the hill. At the intersection, cross very carefully to the convent complex.

5 St Norbert's Convent

The Premonstratensians owned the nearby town and its surrounding fields from its founding in 1162 until it was handed over to the city of Krakow in 1910. On Easter Monday the streets around the convent are caught up in the Emaus street festival. Part of the fun is a water battle. A leftover of ancient fertility rites, males (especially adolescents) are expected to soak females (especially young, single and attractive ones) and vice versa. Anything from water pistols or squirt-guns to buckets is considered fair play.

Crumbling, but still beautiful, villas on ul. Gontyna

Young Poland

While important political decisions were made in far-off cities, Młoda Polska (Young Poland movement) reigned in Krakow's studios, galleries and salons from 1890 to 1918. It was a local variant on the pan-European style known as Art Nouveau, the Secession or Jugenstil, deeply infused with National Romanticism about the long-lost Polish kingdom.

However, Młoda Polska was very much open to influences from beyond Polish lands. Stanisław Przybyszewski (1868–1927), one of its most visible figureheads, devoured the works of Nietzsche and Freud. Taking to heart the tendency of psychoanalysis to reduce all human activity to thinly clothed sexual desire, he argued that true artists must

have naked souls. He wrote 'In the beginning there was lust. There was nothing else and everything was in lust … Lust is the original strength of life, the guarantee of eternal evolution, the endless leaving and endless returning, the only essence of existence'. His lifestyle of sex, drugs and excessive alcohol won him considerable infamy, if not artistic renown.

New technology and trade opened up styles and techniques from the entire world to Central European artists. Feliks Jasieński (1861–1926) brought oriental art, especially Japanese woodblock prints, to the attention of Krakow artists. Many in the Austro-Hungarian bureaucracy welcomed the international aspect of Młoda Polska. Similar influences on artists in Vienna, Prague, Budapest and Ljubljana were also creating a cosmopolitan style appropriate to a multi-national empire.

However, the Galician Autonomy (see p115) was a time when Poles reasserted their own history, language and ethnic identity. The subjects of Młoda Polska art were often the glorious lives of Polish kings and saints. Wyspiański (see p123) inherited a particularly warm love for the medieval from his master Matejko, as can be seen in his plays and in stained-glass windows like the one glorifying the Blessed Salomea in the Franciscan Church (see pp41–2).

Polish folk art was held up as a prototype of true national style and an

The Zakopane villas demonstrated Młoda Polska's concern for an integrated approach to all the arts. Krakow artists experimented in a wide variety of materials, not just the traditional 'high' arts like painting and sculpture, but also crafts like textile-weaving and furniture-making. Even a classically trained painter like Józef Mehoffer (1869–1946) could make his name as a stained-glass designer and dabble in interior design.

STANISŁAW WYSPIAŃSKI (1869–1907)

Wyspiański was one of the most startlingly multi-talented people in the history of European culture. He was a playwright, poet, painter and interior designer. While still a student, he assisted his master Jan Matejko (1838–93) in renovating the Kościół Mariacki, beginning his life-long association with churches and medieval history.

Although Wyspiański was nominally a member of the Młoda Polska movement, other artists were unable to reproduce the extreme interdisciplinary originality of his œuvre. His burial in the Crypt of the Worthy (*see p100*) became a demonstration for Polish independence from the occupying forces.

exemplar of the simple beauty of traditional craftsmanship. Stanisław Witkiewicz (1851–1915), a Warsaw painter and architect, got it into his head that the Górale (highlanders) in the Tatry mountains around Zakopane represented the last untainted remnant of the original Polish culture. (In fact, much of the Góral stock had migrated from Romania in about the 14th century.)

Starting in 1892, Witkiewicz designed a series of large, structurally complicated Alpine chalets but decorated them with motifs loosely borrowed from the wooden cottages of the local peasants. Witkiewicz called his new hybrid 'the Zakopane Style'. Soon, other artists were borrowing supposed Góral motifs for everything from graphic art to orchestral music.

Opposite: The Franciscan Church, home to Wyspiański's Blessed Salomea
Above: Jama Michalika, once the preferred lair of Cracovian artists

Nowa Huta and Mogiła

To many Cracovians, Nowa Huta is not part of Krakow. In spite of the fact that they share a single municipal administration, they tend to speak of 'Huta' as if it were a rather distant village. The distance, however, is one of style and aesthetics, not geography.

Kopiec Wandy, legendary burial mound of an ancient princess

The planned workers' community of Nowa Huta lies 10km (6 miles) east of Old Town Krakow, partly overlying the medieval village of Mogiła, and was laid out in 1949. Many Cracovians regarded it as punishment for Krakow's bourgeois values and cold reception of the new order. The communists said Krakow was trapped in 'unproductive daydreams' and the new influx of working-class inhabitants would 'safeguard it from fossilisation'.

The first steel production went on line in 1954 at the Lenin plant and by 1955 the district already had 85,000 inhabitants. Today, the figure is about 250,000 which, whether the artists and philosophers like it or not, is nearly a third of Krakow's population.

Huta im. Tadeusza Sendzimira (Doges' Palace)

Formerly known as Huta im. Lenina, the name was changed to honour Tadeusz Sendzimir (1894–1989), a Polish-American engineer and metallurgist. Technology that he invented is in use in the plant.

The administration buildings by the entrance to the Nowa Huta steelworks (*ul. Ustajek 1*) are locally nicknamed the Doges' Palace due to the elements borrowed from the Italian Renaissance. They are also sometimes known as the Sukiennice because the gables are almost direct quotations from the building on Rynek Główny.

A visit to the steelworks is educational and highly entertaining, but usually requires a reservation at least two weeks in advance. You go with a paid guide who will probably not speak English. Because the plant is so large, you must have some sort of transport to take you from unit to unit. The tourism office can offer you a translator and a minibus for hire.

Nowa Huta

Reservations should be made at PTTK Stalowa 16/2. Tel/fax: (012) 643 7905. You may visit between 9am and 3pm daily.

Kopiec Wandy (Wanda's Mound)

Queen Wanda, daughter of King Krak, is said to have ruled Krakow after her two brothers killed each other in a dispute over the throne. Among the foreign princes who coveted the Wiślan lands was the German Prince Rytgier. When Wanda refused his offer of marriage, Rytgier vowed he would take the city by force. As he gathered his army, Wanda prayed to her gods and offered herself as a sacrifice in exchange for victory. Then she girded herself for battle and led her troops into the field. The Wiślan army was victorious and returned to Krakow to celebrate. Queen Wanda, however, put on a white linen robe and a wreath of flowers. After giving all her goods to her people, she threw herself into the Wisła river and drowned. Her body washed ashore far to the east of the city. The mound raised on that spot was named Mogiła (Tomb) in her honour.

Although a thorough archaeological investigation has never been made, it is assumed that Wanda's Mound is roughly the same age as Krak's Mound or a little earlier. Early medieval records all name the area as a tomb, indicating that the kernel of the legend is very old. In the 19th century, the story took on

The Cistercian Abbey at Mogiła

nationalistic overtones and the legendary queen is often referred to as 'Wanda-Who-Didn't-Want-A-German'.

In 1890, a monument with a red marble base and a white eagle was placed at the top of the mound. The plinth is inscribed with Wanda's name and a sword and distaff, recalling the lines by Józef Ignacy Kraszewski (1812–87), 'a girl sits in the capital, a garland instead of a crown, a distaff not a sword she holds, she wants not a husband, she has not a lord!' The white eagle was designed by Matejko.

As work forged forward on Nowa Huta in the late 1950s, Wanda's Mound turned out to be within the area planned for building. It was proposed to dig up the mound and pile it up again somewhere else, but fortunately

White eagle atop Wanda's monument

someone suggested the plans could be changed instead.

Kościół N.M.P. Królowej Polski 'Arka' (B.V.M. Queen of Poland Church 'the Ark')

The communist planners of Nowa Huta did not see any need for churches in their workers' paradise. It took several mass demonstrations and gentle pressure from the Church hierarchy to win permission in 1957 for a new church. A cross was set up, but the start of building constantly delayed. In 1960 the communists reneged on their promise and tried to remove the cross. The resulting protests gave the street its name: Defenders of the Cross. In 1967 Archbishop Karol Wojtyła persuaded the authorities to grant a building permit for a nearby site and the Church of the Blessed Virgin Mary, Queen of Poland was finally consecrated on 15 May 1977.

The rather post-modern church was designed to look like Noah's Ark. Under the boat-shaped roof, there is clear glass representing water; under that, a layer of smooth stones represents the ground. Love it or hate it, Arka leaves a strong impression on its viewers. In a way, Arka became a sort of status symbol for many Polish parishes that built concrete post-modern blobs in the early 1990s next to their Gothic and Baroque churches. It was visible proof that they finally had the power and money to get away with it. *ul. Obrońców Krzyża.*

Opactwo Cystersów (Cistercian Abbey)

The bishop of Krakow brought the Cistercians, the leading edge of

Church of St Bartholomew

ecclesiastical reform and church architecture in their time, to Krakow in 1222. They settled in the little village of Mogiła to the east.

In spite of the Baroque façade, this church has retained its earlier character. The spacious interior reveals the moment when Romanesque transformed into Gothic. It is also decorated with rare 16th-century frescoes.

The church possesses the last of three crucifixes that miraculously floated down the Wisła river one day. When the wild Tartars arrived in 1241 to plunder the abbey, the figure of Jesus on the crucifix gave them such a dirty look that they ran away terrified. In 1259, a braver band of Tartars tried to steal the crucifix but every time they made a grab, some mysterious force pushed their ladder away. When King Kazimierz the Great visited the abbey, the crucifix spoke up and recommended that he donate more money to the church.

Across the street is the Kościół św. Bartolomieja (Church of St Bartholomew), a rare example of 15th-century wooden architecture.

Plac Centralny (Central Square)

At first glance, this wide *étoile*, with its broad boulevards and arcaded *piano nobile*, reveals more of its Renaissance and Baroque heritage than its origin in communist central planning. The square was laid out in 1949 when architecture was still 'national in form and socialist in content'. Instead of the monumental House of Culture that was planned to fill the strangely open side of the square, a low functionalist building, *Nowohuckie Centrum Kultury* (Nowa Huta Culture Centre, commonly known by its initials NCK) was erected during 1974–83.

THE STRANGE FATE OF V I LENIN

A colossal statue of Lenin astride Nowa Huta was unveiled in 1973 on the small square on Al. Róz. It was not appreciated by the local proletariat. On the night of 18 April 1979, steelworkers planted stolen explosives at its base and attempted art criticism of the most extreme sort. They succeeded in blowing out every window on the street. Minus a piece of leg, Lenin survived. In 1989, the local authorities decided to remove the statue but they were pre-empted by local anarchists who tore it down just before the anniversary of Martial Law. Lenin was put in storage until 1992 when he was sold to a Swedish businessman who gave him to a park near Värnamo.

Walk: Nowa Huta and Mogiła

Although it may not be advisable to walk around Huta at night, especially if you are carrying a lot of photographic equipment, a stroll during the day will help visitors get a feel for the grimmer side of the communist legacy.

Allow 2–3 hours.

Nowa Huta was designed on a grand scale. Stock up on a few tram tickets to cover some of the distances between objects of interest. Start the walk at the gates to the steelworks at ul. Ustajek 1.

1 The Doges' Palace

Although tours are only allowed with advance reservation, you can get a feel for the incredible size of the steelworks from the entrance area.

Walk or take a tram one stop south to Wanda's Mound. The mound is on your left, a little hidden by the greenery.

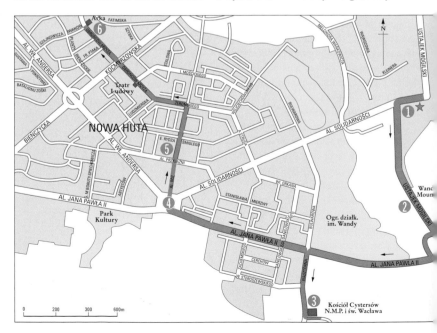

2 Kopiec Wandy

In the 1990s this area looked rather
abandoned, but the city has invested in
some landscaping and repaired the
damage to the monument on top of the
mound (*see p125*). If you were not able
to book a tour of the steelworks, this will
be your best view of its grey expanse.
*Catch a No. 15 tram towards the city
centre. The second stop lets you off at
ul. Klasztorna. Follow Klasztorna on
your left down to the abbey on the
left-hand side of the road.*

3 The Abbey at Mogiła

The Cistercian Abbey at Mogiła is
another reminder of the medieval village
that stood here before the communists
framed Nowa Huta's fearful symmetry
(*see pp127–8*). Across the street is a
wooden Gothic church dedicated to
St Bartholomew.
*Walk back to the main road and
take the tram two stops further to
the monumental Central Square.*

The Ark has landed

4 Plac Centralny

This is the heart of the communist-
planned suburb, built while there was
still some faith in the ideals of Marx
and Lenin (*see p127*). As part of their
efforts to educate the working class,
the communists were careful to include
a great number of bookshops, reading
rooms and libraries in their plans for
Nowa Huta.
*Pass through the most central pair of
buildings into the pedestrian walkway
that is the start of Al. Róż.*

5 Al. Róż (Boulevard of Roses)

The buildings on Al. Róż represent the
height of pseudo-Renaissance ornament
on Socialist Realist buildings. The rose
garden in the centre of the small square
once held a gigantic statue of Lenin
(*see p127*). Continue straight ahead to
Al. Przyjaźni and on to ul. Żeromskiego
and then turn left.

On your left, exotic influences
can be clearly seen in the design
by Janusz Ingarden (*b.* 1923) of
Teatr Ludowy (People's Theatre, *os.
Teatralnym 34*). The theatre opened
with Bogusławski's opera *Krakowiacy
i Górale* (*The Cracovians and the
Highlanders*), which gave the names
to the housing estates opposite.
*Cross the busy ul. Kocmyrzowska
to where the street continues as
ul. Obrońców Krzyża. Just past a
small market, you come to Arka.*

6 Arka

The shocking bulk of the Arka church
(*see p126*) has become a symbol of the
Roman Catholic Church's triumph over
communism.

In 1932, the Soviet *Literaturnaya Gazeta* declared that 'the masses demand of an artist honesty, truthfulness, and a revolutionary, socialist realism in the representation of the proletarian revolution'. It was the grey dawn of one of the least-loved artistic movements in the history of Europe.

At no point in its 57-year history did Socialist Realism have a clearly defined aesthetic programme. It tended towards relatively simple and traditional techniques with realistic, easy-to-recognise images. The main unifying factor in Socialist Realism was its ideological content. Anything that glorified the existing regime and the role of the worker could qualify.

Poland unwillingly joined the Communist Bloc when it was liberated by Soviet troops in 1945. Of Poland's major cultural centres, Krakow had emerged from the war with the least damage. There was little space for major new buildings or monuments in the Old Town or suburbs. The epicentre of uncompromising communist urban planning shifted to Nowa Huta.

Socialist Realist buildings of the 1940s and 1950s were 'national in form and socialist in content'. Notions of a utopian workers' community dictated the function of architecture. Each unit of housing in Nowa Huta was supplied

with a calculated number of schools, libraries, workers' canteens and health services. However, the architectural forms continued to be Polish.

The monumental complex around Plac Centralny (Central Square) was amongst the first erected in Nowa Huta. Designed by Tadeusz Ptaszycki (1908–80), the handsome grey arcades with their strong Renaissance and Classicist influences are reminders that Nowa Huta was intended to reward the workers, not to punish them. Other noteworthy Huta buildings from this period are the 'Doges' Palace' (*see p124*) and Teatr Ludowy (*see p129*).

One of the more interesting examples of 1950s Socialist Realism outside Nowa Huta is Józef Gołąb's design for the Miastoprojekt building (*ul. Kraszewskiego 36*). The dignified classical symmetry of its walls once housed the architects who planned Nowa Huta.

The whole Communist Bloc experienced unrest in the mid-1950s.

As part of the resulting crackdown, local and national styles were replaced by bland, international functionalism. Buildings were increasingly prefabricated. Whole housing estates might consist of one layout of flats repeated to the horizon. One of the very few buildings to wring an interesting effect out of an inherently drab system was Bohdan Lisowski's Dom o Stu Balkonach (House of 100 Balconies – ul. Retoryka 4), which uses an offset zigzag pattern.

As communism began to show cracks, Socialist Realism even sprouted examples of Post-modernism. Next to the increasingly shoddy prefab houses in Nowa Huta, Wojciech Pietrzyk's 'Arka' (*ul. Obrońców Krzyża 1*, built 1967–77) depicts Noah's Ark landing on the roof of the blob-shaped church.

When communism came tumbling down at the end of the 1980s, most of the easily removed monuments vanished overnight. Bronze plaques that declared 'Lenin slept here' were melted down. The grandiose statue in Nowa Huta (*see p127*) was sold to a businessman. Today, only the grim housing estates remain to show that the 'proletarian revolution' ever muddied the clear waters of Krakow's art and architecture.

Opposite top: Egyptian influences at Teatr Ludowy
Opposite bottom: Socialist Realism statue
Above: 'The Ark' church in Nowa Huta

Excursions

Auschwitz-Birkenau State Museum in Oświęcim

The Auschwitz-Birkenau State Museum is a grim destination and afterwards you will want some time to contemplate what you have seen. The exhibits are designed to provoke a strong emotional response to one of the blackest crimes in European history. The museum is **not** appropriate for children under the age of 14.

'Auschwitz' has become a symbol of the Holocaust and Nazi war crimes as a whole. Contrary to popular opinion, it was not the deadliest of the Nazi death camps. Its fame is in part due to the inmates, including writers like Tadeusz Borowski (1922–51) and Elie Weisel (*b.* 1928), who survived to tell their grisly tale. However, Auschwitz-Birkenau combined all the different functions of the Nazi camps: prisoner-of-war camp, concentration camp, work camp and death camp.

Although the exact numbers are not known, the vast majority of the camp's

'Work will set you free' – the gate to Auschwitz I

victims were indubitably there simply because they were Jews. Auschwitz, however, also held many other inmates: gypsies, communists, homosexuals, Polish intellectuals and political prisoners, priests and criminals, as well as Soviet prisoners of war.

Soviet soldiers were the first to be killed with Zyklon B in experimental gas chambers. Later, the gas was mostly used on Jewish victims. Many who survived the gas chambers were shot, starved, worked to death, experimented on or otherwise killed by the harsh conditions in the camp. Most historians believe that between 1.1 and 1.5 million prisoners were killed at Auschwitz-Birkenau. The Nazi camp operated from 1940 until its liberation by Soviet troops in 1945.

The museum includes two sections of the camps: the brick buildings at Auschwitz I (mostly for political prisoners and prisoners of war) and the immense concentration and death camp at Auschwitz II-Birkenau (mostly for Jews and gypsies). During the summer, there is a bus between the two sites. It would take about two days to visit the entire area of the museum that is open to visitors. Most people find that three hours is about enough. It is advisable to visit with a guided group or engage a private guide; most of the exhibits are marked with explanations in several languages but a guide can answer questions and direct you to areas of special interest. Do not miss the black-and-white film about the liberation of the camp (showings in English, French, German and Japanese) in the reception building. Encourage your guide to show you the *Sauna* (pronounced 'zow-na' – the central baths) at Birkenau. It is the last thing on most tours and exhausted visitors sometimes overlook this extremely well-crafted exhibit. Some displays, such as the one in Block 13 dedicated to Roma gypsies or the rotating exhibition of art in Block 12, do not usually make it into the guided tours but are well worth coming back for. You can buy guidebooks and glossy picture albums in the museum gift shop, as well as flowers and candles if you feel moved to leave a memorial. The canteen serves heavy Polish food. Visitors with special dietary needs should bring a packed meal.

There are two bus routes from Krakow to Oświęcim. The service run by PKS-Wadowice leaves the main bus station (corner of ul. Worcella and ul. Pawia) at 9am and will drop you off at the museum

entrance about 1hr 45mins later. The
PKS-Oświęcim service departs from a
bus stop on the other side of the railway
station (ul. Bosacka) about once an hour
starting at 7.30am and will drop you off
1hr 30mins later, a short walk from the
museum. Remember that the bus stops at
the town of Oświęcim before it reaches
the museum. The train is more expensive
and stops only in the town, leaving you
to take a local bus or taxi to the museum.
Because the museum closes at 7pm and
you need **at least** 2 hours to make even a
cursory visit to the site, you should leave
Krakow no later than 3pm. Wear
sensible shoes and prepare for changes
in the weather. Most of your visit will
mean walking outdoors. The Auschwitz-
Birkenau State Museum is open all year
round and admission is free. Tel: (033)
843 2133, 844 8102. Open: Jun–Aug,
8am–7pm; May & Sept 6pm; Apr & Oct
5pm; Mar & Nov–Dec 15, 4pm; Dec
16–Feb, 3pm. Archives, library open:
8am–2pm weekdays.

Many Jewish arrivals in Auschwitz-Birkenau were
sent straight to the gas chamber

Above and opposite: the abbey at Tyniec

Most tourists rush straight to the
museum without ever visiting the small,
industrial town of Oświęcim, only 3km
(2 miles) away. Before the Nazis came,
7,000 of Oświęcim's 12,300 residents
were Jewish. Its Haberfeld kosher vodka
distillery was famous throughout Central
Europe. Although the Great Synagogue
was burnt down in 1941, the smaller
Chevra Lomdei Mishnayot synagogue
survived and now houses the Auschwitz
Jewish Centre.
Plac Ks. Jana Skarbka 3. Tel: (033) 844
7002. Open: Apr–Sept, Sun–Fri
8.30am–8pm; Oct–Mar, Sun–Fri
8.30am–6pm. Closed: all Jewish
holidays.

Tyniec
The Benedictine abbey at Tyniec was
probably founded about 1044 by King
Kazimierz I the Restorer on the site
of a prehistoric fortress, on a limestone
outcrop above the Wisła river. With
its undisputed command of the plain
upstream of Krakow, its function was

always military as well as religious. Romanesque elements show through in many abbey walls, and fragments of defences from the 14th century onwards are still visible around the hill.

Legend claims that earlier on this spot was the castle of the pagan lord, Walter the Strong. Walter captured the Wiślan king, Wiesław the Handsome, in battle and locked him in his dungeon. However, while he was away, Walter's beautiful but fickle wife Helgund freed the comely monarch and ran off with him to Wiesław's castle at Wiślica. Walter stormed his rival's castle while Wiesław was hunting in the forest. Using her womanly wiles, however, Helgund managed to convince her husband that she had been unwillingly kidnapped. Under the pretext of hiding him from the returning king, she led her husband into a trap. Wiesław ordered Walter to be manacled to the wall of his bedroom and then proceeded to cuckold the enraged knight right before his eyes.

Wiesław the Handsome had an unmarried sister, Rynga the Ugly. Rynga felt sorry for poor Walter and offered to slip him a sword if he would agree to

The synagogue at Oświęcim

marry her. Walter agreed and the next time that his wife and her paramour put on a show for him, Walter the Strong burst free of his manacles and snatched the sword from its hiding place. With a single, mighty stroke of the sword he removed his rival and made himself eligible for a second marriage.

Tyniec is about 12km (7½ miles) west of the centre of Krakow. It is an easy drive from Rynek Dębnicki or just take the No. 112 city bus.
ul. Benedyktyńska 37.

Wieliczka

No trip to Krakow would be complete without a visit to the unforgettable salt mines in Wieliczka. Although they are the oldest mines in the world still open, absolutely no knowledge of Polish history is needed to appreciate them. The tour involves a lot of walking underground so very young children and the elderly may wish to avoid it. A small portion of the tour is wheelchair-accessible but you will need to pay extra for the lift. Remember that it remains a constant 15°C (59°F) all year round in the mines and dress accordingly.

As the primordial seas that covered this area dried up, they left thick deposits of rock salt. Humans, who arrived millennia later, quickly discovered the flavouring and preservative qualities of this valuable substance. They collected salt from the rocks and pools on the surface from at least 3000 BC.

In the Middle Ages, the locals learnt to dig down to the uppermost portions of the salt deposits in open pits. The first known mines are from AD 1280, shortly

The spirit of the mines invites you

after the arrival of Princess Kinga in Krakow.

Legend claims that when Princess Kinga (Kunegunda) of Hungary (1234–92) was betrothed to King Bolesław V the Bashful, she took a ring off her hand and threw it down a Hungarian salt mine, declaring that her dowry would be salt. Shortly after her wedding in Krakow, the new queen travelled to Wieliczka and ordered the locals to start digging for her dowry. When they struck rock, they chipped off a piece and handed it to her. It was pure rock salt and her ring was found miraculously suspended within it.

The historical reality seems to have been that Princess Kinga brought experienced salt miners and engineers in her retinue from Hungary. Her husband Bolesław put royal patronage behind the mining operations at Wieliczka and nearby Bochnia. Within a few generations, salt production accounted for nearly a third of the royal income. Trade in salt was a major driver of the local economy and encouraged the development of infrastructure along the trade route from Wieliczka to Kazimierz to Krakow.

Today, the easiest way to get to Wieliczka from Krakow is take one of the minibuses that leaves every ten minutes from the front of the railway station (*ul. Worcella*). There are also regular PKS buses and trains.

Wieliczka has more than 350km (215 miles) of tunnels, of which only 2km (1¼ miles) are part of the tourist track. You can buy tickets to see just the mines, or both mines and museum. Although the underground museum is fascinating, most visitors are just too tired to be interested by the time they get there.

You must see the mines with a guide. If a tour in English is not available when you visit, just buy the small guidebook in English and follow a Polish-language tour. The guides repeat the text almost word-for-word.

Most visitors are surprised to discover that Wieliczka salt is a dirty grey when it is in large blocks. It only becomes white when it forms smaller crystals, such as the salty stalactites that appear on any object left in the mines near a source of moisture. The guide will tell you not to lick the walls. Someone in your group will do it anyway!

Another surprise is that the miners occasionally succumbed to artistic urges, carving odd figures in the salt. At first, they tended to be simple religious shrines suitable for men working at a dangerous job. The Chapel of St Kinga, however, is a full-blown underground church in which everything from the altar to the chandeliers is carved entirely

from salt. In communist times, the workers were encouraged to carve more secular subjects, leading to a collection of salt-mining dwarves frozen in the middle of their work.

The miners like to joke that the salt keeps them well preserved. There is a certain truth to their jest: the mines contain unusually clean and bacteria-free air. At a level below the one that tourists visit, there is a small hospital for respiratory disorders. *Tel: (012) 278 7302, 278 7366. www.cyf-kr.edu.pl/wieliczka. Open: 16 Apr–15 Oct, 8am–6pm; 16 Oct–15 Apr, 8am–4pm.*

Zakopane

The sleepy mountain village of Zakopane was discovered in the 1870s by the urban intelligentsia of Poland. They flocked here in droves to get away from Warsaw and Krakow. Fashionable spas and bohemian artists' colonies suddenly sprung up. The newcomers invented a style of villas that better suited their needs than the locals' humble wooden huts and congratulated themselves on participating in the last unspoiled remnant of authentic Polish culture (*see p123*).

About 1906, skiing arrived in Zakopane, creating a whole new industry for the region. The first hardy tourists to try the sport in Poland had to hike three hours up the mountain in order to slide back down using a single stick between their legs as a brake. It was not until the 1930s that ski lifts came into use here. By the 1950s, it had become a mass-market sport and a major source of income for the town.

Getting to Zakopane by car can be quite a challenge, especially in the skiing season when the narrow road from Krakow becomes an unending traffic jam. Parking places can be difficult to find in Zakopane during the season. Most visitors will be happier taking the trains and buses that run several times a day from Krakow.

Zakopane has a modest but enchanting wooden church on ul. Kościeliska built during 1847–51, before the influx of outsiders. Its crowded cemetery contains many early Zakopane-enthusiasts, including Witkiewicz, inventor of the

Zakopane Style. His villas, though their interiors are usually not open to the public, are worth walking around to see, especially the influential Dom Pod Jedlami (House Under the Firs) built during 1896–7. Every detail of the house and furnishings was designed by Witkiewicz or his collaborators as part of an organic whole.

For many visitors, the most attractive thing about Zakopane will be leaving it on a hike up into the mountains. A popular destination is Morskie Oko (Eye of the Sea), a circular lake high in the mountains, which is supposed to be so

Mountain views and fresh air

deep that it connects with the sea via an underground passage. If you want the view without the strenuous hike, you may take the funicular up Gubalówka.

Skiing in Zakopane is famous in Poland, but may leave foreign visitors underwhelmed. In spite of boasting the largest number of lifts in the country, the runs are short and overcrowded by most European standards. During the season, accommodation is hard to come by and all services are painfully dear. In recent times Italy and Slovakia have become more attractive alternatives for Polish skiers.

Shopping is every bit as much part of the Zakopane experience as hiking or skiing. The main shopping street, ul. Krupówki, offers a predictable selection of cheap restaurants and mass-produced authentic folk art. The bazaar at the lower end of the street near the Gubalówka funicular contains even more goods for sale (wooden spoons, woollen socks, whole sheepskins, sheep cheese) but remember to bargain or you may end up paying a lot more.

Shopping on Krupówki, Zakopane's other sport

Oscypki: Highlander Smoked Cheese

In 2002, a wave of shock and horror rolled down from the mountains and across Krakow. Someone had suggested that new EU laws might make the highlanders' famous sheep cheese, *oscypek*, illegal. This ancient Polish provender, this untrammelled symbol of national identity, would not pass muster with the heartless bureaucracy in Brussels.

The turmoil subsided only when word was passed back into the hills that the *oscypki* were safe. EU rules protecting French farmers' unpasteurised cheeses would also cover the Polish highlanders' cheese. Culinary revolution was narrowly avoided.

The Górale (highlanders) had reason to fear. Under communism their beloved cheese had, in fact, been illegal. Not only was *oscypek* produced without state hygiene and production standards, but the whole idea of cottage industry had reeked of capitalism. Another issue recently raised was that of local officials from the Podhale region trying to patent the name 'Oscypek'. This was seen as an act of hijacking local tradition and the Polish highlanders were incensed. The officials withdrew their request although the issue remains unresolved.

Real, unadulterated Góral *oscypki* are made with 100 per cent unpasteurised sheep cheese, salted and pressed into carved wooden forms, usually in a lozenge shape. The precise procedures of its production are closely guarded family secrets, passed on from generation to generation. Most *oscypki* are then lovingly smoked to a warm, orangey-yellow colour and rich, woody aroma. Lesser sorts are sometimes made with a mixture of cow cream. There are even counterfeits on the market made entirely of other dairy products.

Related varieties include *bundz* (moist, spongy, white sheep cheese with a slightly sour taste) and *bryndza* (spreadable white sheep cheese with a rich, tangy flavour).

While there is a certain thrill to buying your *oscypki* from the little old ladies who sell them on Floriańska in Krakow or Krupówki in Zakopane, the safest bet is to stock up at the shop above Pod Aniołami restaurant at *ul. Grodzka 15* in Krakow. And remember, regardless of what Brussels may think, you should not try to take unpasteurised cheeses across international borders.

Pieczony Oscypki

Baked Oscypki is a local favourite. Cut the cheese into slices and brown on a very hot pan or grill. Do not add any oil. These cheeses do not run while being baked. Serve with fresh bread. Delicious. Alternatively, slice uncooked, and eat (preferably with a glass of vodka).

Opposite: Selling *Oscypki* on the streets
Below: Smoked and unsmoked varieties in several sizes

Skansen Budownictwa
Ludowego

Getting Away From It All

The varied countryside around Krakow offers abundant opportunity to get away from the dirty city. There are several national parks in the area which cover forests, rivers and rolling hills. Rock climbers will enjoy the many cliffs and spelunkers (potholers) will find the local limestone particularly rich in caves.

Las Wolski (Wolski Woods)
A huge expanse of natural woodland covering 422ha (1,000 acres) of hilly ground west of the city, Las Wolski contains many leafy paths in addition to Krakow's zoo.

Skansen Budownictwa Ludowego (Skansen of Folk Architecture)
A very small *skansen* (outdoor museum of vernacular architecture) stands at the northern edge of the park. There are three wooden buildings: a church and two granaries. The spooky-looking church is an accurate reconstruction of an early 16th-century church that burnt down in 1978. The exterior is late Gothic; the interior is Baroque.
Buses: 102, 152.

Klasztor Kamedułów na Bielanach (Camaldolese Monastery at Bielany)
The church was started in 1609 but the steep hillside required expensive engineering work to lay the foundations. The white Baroque church was not ready for consecration to the Assumption of the Most Holy Virgin Mary until 1642.

Legend claims that Sebastian Lubomirski, the previous owner of the hill, had no intention of letting the monks have it. Mikołaj Wolski, the monks' patron, invited Lubomirski and many of his peers to a huge feast where he described the difficulties involved in finding a suitable spot for the monastery. Lubomirski was shamed into signing over the land and in thanks Wolski gave him the set of silver plates used at the feast. The hill was thereafter known as 'Silver Mountain'.

The monks are anchorites, essentially hermits who live together but in separate cells under very strict rules of silence and seclusion. They normally do not even meet each other except for prayers and mass. Women are allowed in the church 12 times a year for religious holidays. No visitors are allowed into the anchorites' quarters behind the church. At Pentecost, the church hosts a traditional festival that draws crowds from Krakow.
In summer you can reach it via the Wisła ferry. Otherwise, buses 109, 209, 229, 239, 249, 259 and 269, all leaving from Salwator.

Panieńskie Skałki (Maidens' Cliffs)
Since 1953, the valley below the Maidens' Cliffs has been a strict nature reserve for a number of endangered

Kopiec Kościuszki

shovels that volunteers could use once and then take home as a souvenir, and a post office, so postcards could be sent home stamped 'Piłsudski Mound'.

Piłsudski's memory was not cherished by the communists. In 1953, the plaque on top of the mound was pulled down by army tanks and the mound was left to grow wild. It disappeared from many maps and tourist guides.

Thanks to veteran soldiers and the Solidarity movement, the mound was given a perfunctory tidying in 1980. In 1991 Piłsudski's Mound was thoroughly renovated and the memorial plaque returned to the summit.

species of trees and flowers. It is illegal to gather any wildlife here.
(*See The Legend of the Maidens' Cliffs on this page.*)

Kopiec Piłsudskiego (Piłsudski Mound)

The largest of Krakow's earth mounds was begun in 1934, under the title of Kopiec Niepodległości Marszałka Józefa Piłsudskiego – Mogiły Mogił (Freedom Mound of Marshal Józef Piłsudskiego – Tomb of Tombs), to honour the 20th anniversary of Piłsudski's daring march from Krakow to Warsaw, which led to Polish independence. Over 3,500 urns of earth from graves or battlefields important to Poland's rebirth were buried in the mound.

When the much-loved dictator died in 1935, the mound became a cenotaph to Piłsudski himself. Thousands of volunteers came from all over Poland. The site had booths, selling engraved

Zoo

The first menagerie in Krakow was King Jagiełło's pride of lions in 1406, but a zoological park for the public did not arrive until 1895. The current zoo was founded in 1929 on a hill in the

---

THE LEGEND OF THE MAIDENS' CLIFFS

The cliffs are named after the nuns who escaped from their convent in Zwierzyniec (see p116) via a secret underground passage during the Tartar raid of 1421. The Tartars discovered their escape and hunted them down, intent on ravishing the undefended maidens. However, the Virgin Mary heard their prayers and the cliffs opened up to offer them sanctuary, slamming shut in the faces of the lust-driven Tartars. Some say the nuns are there still. If you listen very carefully you can hear them singing their hymns deep inside the rock.

middle of Las Wolski. The zoo focuses mostly on local species like bison, wild boar, deer and lynx but there is also a smattering of exotic beasts like monkeys and yaks.

Open: daily in summer, 9am–6pm; autumn and spring, 9am–5pm; winter, 9am–4pm. Bus: 134. Admission charge.

Ojcowski Park Narodowy (Ojców National Park)

This is one of the largest and most diverse parks in the area, 2,145ha (5,300 acres) of rocky and wooded terrain in a 12-km (7½ mile) stretch of the Prądnik river valley, offering visitors picturesque castles and churches, lush wildlife and spectacular views.

The river has carved the limestone into a variety of fantastic shapes. The most famous is Maczuga Herkulesa (Hercules' Club), a tower of rock precariously balanced with the wide end up and the narrow end down. Legend claims that it was set like this by the unearthly powers of Pan Twardowski (*see p63*). It is near Pieskowa Skała castle on the well-marked red trail.

Ojców also boasts about 210 caves, only a few of which are open to casual tourists. The most famous is the 270-m (885-ft) Grota Łokietka (Elbow-High's Grotto). In 1300, King Vaclav II of Bohemia conquered Krakow and declared himself King of Poland. The runner-up, Prince Władysław Łokietek (the Elbow-High) had to flee. With Vaclav's troops in hot pursuit, Łokietek and a few loyal knights made for the rough, wooded terrain along the Prądnik river. As the enemy closed in, the story is that Łokietek and his men dived into a

cave for their last stand. The Bohemian troops, however, walked right past it. When the danger had passed, the puzzled prince found that a spider had built a huge web across the cave entrance in just a few seconds. The Bohemians took this to mean that no-one had entered the cave for days. *The cave is open 9.30am– 6pm in summer, shorter hours at other times of year.*

Grodzisko

Halfway between the town of Ojców and the castle at Pieskowa Skała (*see pp145–6*), a limestone promontory 30m (100ft) above the valley floor supports a small Baroque church. Legend makes

A chapel 'not built on the land of Ojców'

this the convent where the Blessed Salomea (1211–68) died. For five days her corpse lay in state, emitting a strange and beautiful perfume that lifted the nuns to new levels of religious ardour. It was later moved to the Franciscan Church in Krakow (*see pp41–2*), again in an odour of sanctity.

The church was designed in a rather quirky Baroque style by Sebastian Piskorski (1636–1707), a professor and rector of the Jagiellonian University. One of the strangest decorations is the remnant of a Baroque fountain depicting an elephant carrying an obelisk on its back, a symbol of wisdom. It is obviously a copy of the famous monument near the Pantheon in Rome. The original, designed by Gian Lorenzo Bernini (a friend of Piskorski's), was based on the enigmatic and controversial Hypnerotomachia Poliphili (Poliphil's Love-Strife Dream) from 1499.

Ojców

There are only ruins of the mighty Gothic fortress raised here by Kazimierz the Great in the 14th century. He named the castle in honour of his father (*ojciec*) Władysław Łokietek, who holed up in the nearby cliffs during the Bohemian occupation. The castle was badly damaged by the Swedish 'Deluge' in 1655, but it was partly rebuilt and hosted the last king of Poland, Stanisław Poniatowski, during his tour of the highlands. In the 1820s Ojców castle fell into ruin and was largely dismantled by its owner in 1829. However, the picturesque gatehouse still rubs shoulders with the natural cliff and the massive limestone walls of the keep (eight-sided

on the outside, six-sided on the inside) stand as steadfast as the day they were built.

The town below has many pretty chalets and a fine public park, reminders of the days when Ojców was a popular spa. One of the town's unique charms is Kaplica Na Wodzie (Chapel on the Water), built in 1901 when Ojców was in Russian Poland. Tsar Nicholas II had ordered a moratorium on building new chapels 'on the land of Ojców'. By building the chapel on a bridge over water, the Poles got around the law.

The chapel's style is sometimes patriotically called 'styl ojcowski' (Ojców Style, analogous to the Zakopane Style, *see p123*). *Chapel open: 10am–4.45pm.*

Pieskowa Skała

The name of this castle either comes from Peszko, a pet form of Piotr/Peter, or perhaps the shape of the rock once suggested a dog – *piesek*. Kazimierz the Great rebuilt a palisade fortress in stone in the 14th century. The castle was given to nobleman Piotr Szafraniec by Kazimierz's successor, King Louis d'Anjou the Hungarian, for supporting Louis' somewhat uncertain claim to the Polish throne.

According to legend, Szafraniec was addicted to alchemy. To fund his experiments, he would offer rich merchants a night's lodging in the safety of his castle. After a heavy meal and strong wine, the sleepy guest would be shown to a dark doorway that led, not to their bedroom, but to a deep pit. Szafraniec could then loot the merchant's goods at his leisure.

In another story, a beautiful young girl named Dorotka was given in marriage to another Lord Szafraniec. Because she would not consent, he locked her in the high tower that once stood above the castle. However, her true love disguised himself as a monk in order to get into the tower to rescue her. Unfortunately, they were caught in the act. The vengeful Lord Szafraniec locked the girl in the tower to die of starvation and ordered her lover to be trampled to death by horses below her window.

Skały Twardowskiego

Starting in 1542, the Szafraniec family rebuilt the old Gothic castle as a Renaissance palace, often known as the Little Wawel because of its arcaded courtyard. Burnt and bombarded many times, Pieskowa Skała was falling into ruin until conservation work started in the 20th century. Today the castle hosts a branch of the Wawel Museum displaying European art from the Middle Ages to the Baroque.
ul. Sułoszowa 4. Tel: (012) 389 6004. Open: May–Sept, Tue–Fri 10am–3.30pm, Sat–Sun and holidays 11am–5.30pm; Oct–Apr, Tue–Fri 10am–3.30pm.

Skały Twardowskiego
The white limestone crags of Skały Twardowskiego (Twardowski's Cliffs) rise southwest of the city. Around their base is scrub with an amazing variety of trees and bushes, giving way to wetland grasses and reeds in lower-lying areas. Paths – some flat, others quite steep – meander through the park. The brisk climb to the top is rewarded with spectacular views across Krakow.

Rock-climbers are particularly fond of the sheer drops. On warm weekends the limestone seems alive with human ants scampering up and down the rock face. There are short and long climbs, at all skill levels.

The central portion of the cliffs was hollowed out by quarrying. After that stopped at the end of the 1980s, water filtered through the porous limestone, creating a large lake. The crystal-clear water and dramatic cliffs attract scuba divers all year long. Apart from that, swimming in the lake is supposedly

The lake at Skały Twardowskiego

forbidden (there is no lifeguard), but the hot summers bring Cracovians to its cold waters in droves.

Military enthusiasts can explore Austro-Hungarian artillery emplacements at the northeastern edge of the cliffs, overlooking the river. Their outlines are clearly visible under the grass. Below are several small caves, including the short Jaskinia Jasna (Bright cave) and the 500-m (1,640-ft) maze of Grota Twardowskiego (Twardowski's Grotto), where the wizard (*see p63*) is said to have practised his black magic. None of these caves has been prepared for tourist visits, so bring appropriate equipment if you plan to explore.
Trams: 18, 19, 22; Bus: 124.

Spływ Dunajcem (Rafting Down the Dunajec)
One of the most popular excursions in the mountains near Krakow is a leisurely drift down the placid Dunajec river. It is sometimes over-enthusiastically billed as 'white-water adventure' but there is no danger. Nonetheless, the natural beauty of the steep cliffs plunging into the water will take your breath away.

The towns of Sromowce Niżne and Kąty (*buses from the main Krakow bus station*) are the most popular places to start your voyage. Alternatively, private bus companies offer package tours that include pick-up at the hotel, rafting and return to Krakow.

Most tourists opt for local highlanders to pole their *tratwa* (raft) gently down the stream. Canoes and rubber pontoons are sometimes available. Remember that you will be trapped on a raft in the middle of a river for over an hour. Bring rainwear.

The Tatry mountains

Shopping

In the 14th century, Krakow was one of the few inland members of the mighty Hanseatic League that dominated commerce on the North Sea and Baltic Sea. Today, Tartars and Dutchmen are gone from the Rynek but the spirit of capitalism lives on.

Just a sample of the commodities for sale in Krakow

What to Buy

Krakow offers the traveller a good selection of gifts and souvenirs to take back home. Amber and silver jewellery from the north are still relatively cheap in the south of Poland. Polish poster art is well known for its high standards, although these are difficult to transport home. Linen cloth is still produced in quantity and quality in Poland. The carefully hand-embroidered tablecloths found in many shops around the Rynek make excellent wedding gifts. Woodcarving is particularly common and one of the most popular items is a Góral chess set. Another hit from the mountains are the Góral leather house-slippers. For an original gift, you can browse the music stores for highbrow modern serious music like Penderecki or the pop-folk fusion of Golec uOrkiestra.

Antiques

Tempting as it might be to pick up some of the cheap antiques on the market in Poland, it is illegal to export any work of art produced before 1945. Do not even buy modern copies that might look like an authentic antique if you are not going to be able to prove that it is legal to export. This ban includes printed materials like books.

Bookshops
EMPiK

Four storeys of periodicals, books, music and videos in several languages. *Rynek Główny 5. Tel: (012) 433 1185. www.empik.pl. Open: 10am–10pm Mon–Sat, until 8pm Sun.*

Hetmańska

The shop ceiling is a historic monument in its own right. *Rynek Główny 17. Tel: (012) 430 2453.*

Księgarnia Massolit

An obscure literary reference in its name, thousands of books in English (especially on Central and Eastern Europe), coffee and carrot cake. Worth looking for. *ul. Felicjanek 4.*

Department Stores
Elefant

A mix of the elegant and the tawdry: clothes, footwear, eyewear and novelty gifts. A tailor is on 'emergency repair duty' during business hours. *ul. Podwale 6–7. Tel: (012) 422 6741. Open: Mon–Fri 10am–7pm, Sat 10am–3pm.*

Galeria Centrum

A communist chain successfully moving upmarket: perfumes, toiletries, clothes and an interesting alcohol boutique in the cellar. *ul. św. Anny 2. Tel: (012) 422 9822.*

Jubilat

Possibly the ugliest building in Krakow. Food shopping downstairs, all other domestic needs upstairs. *Al. Słowackiego 64. Tel: (012) 422 3033.*

Hypermarkets

Polish consumers have developed a taste for huge hypermarkets on the French and German model. You should be able to purchase anything from any of the hypermarkets below.

Carrefour

ul. Zakopiańska 62. Tel: (012) 261 7100.

Géant

Al. Bora-Komorowskiego 37. Tel: (012) 617 0600.

Tesco

ul. Kapelanka 54. Tel: (012) 293 2500.

Music

Besides trying EMPiK (*opposite*), look in:

Music Corner

Rynek Główny 13, ul. św. Jana. Tel: (012) 421 8253.

Shopping is a popular pastime

Posters

Galeria Autorska Andrzeja Mleczki

Not just posters but also postcards, mugs and shirts from Krakow's most famous contemporary cartoonist. Some cartoons may be a bit shocking.
ul. św. Jana 14. Tel: (012) 421 7104.

Galeria Plakatu

Original and often surprising film, theatre and festival posters.
ul. Stolarska 8-10. Tel: (012) 421 2640.

Souvenirs

The prices in the stalls inside the Sukiennice are not as bad as you might think and the selection is unbeatable. You can also try:

Sukiennice

Just off the main square. A good selection of folksy knick-knacks.
ul. Bracka 11. Tel: (012) 430 2104.

Wines & Spirits

In addition to the hypermarkets, try:

Baryłeczka

ul. Szczepańska 9. Tel: (012) 429 6267.

Novex

pl. Szczepański 8. Tel: (012) 421 2179 ext. 31.

Szambelan

ul. Golebia 2. Tel: (012) 430 2409. Open: Mon–Sat 10am–8.30pm, Sun 11am–3pm.

Downstairs under the Galeria Centrum department store. Choose from a variety of alcohols and pick the bottle that you would like it in. The staff will gift-wrap your choice and put an excise sticker on it to prove its legality.

Linen

Cool to the touch, linen is one of humanity's oldest fabrics and yet is still eagerly sought by fashion designers to create a 'modern' look. Linen is made from the strong but flexible inner fibre of the long, straight stalks of the flax plant. Before it can be spun as thread, the flax must be repeatedly soaked and pounded to remove the outer layers and soften it.

Since the early Middle Ages, Poland has been a major producer of flax and linen. In June and July, the fields in the Polish countryside are covered with its tiny blue flowers. As the poet Janina Porazińska (1888–1971) put it, 'one heaven above, a second heaven below'.

As the flax ripens at the end of summer, the seeds in their little spherical fruit become an important source of oil and feed for livestock. It is such an important crop that some of the ancient Slavic tribes used it as money.

The harvest and processing of linen was swathed in folk tradition, superstition and magic. According to Zakopane folk-artist Adam Słowiński, the Górale then still had goddesses of linen. His mother told him 'in my village, Ząb, women carried flax to a certain stream where it was known that the goddesses sit. They would leave the flax and some food and, later, after a few days, they would come back and the flax would be spun into linen thread by the goddesses'. This divine linen

was supposed to be unusually fine and even.

The natural properties of linen seem almost miraculous. It is insect-repellent, mildly anti-bacterial and anti-fungal. Made into clothes, it is naturally cool against the skin. It is stronger than cotton and more resistant to wear and tear.

The main reason that linen is not used more often in the hurried modern lifestyle is that it wrinkles easily. If you buy linen, remember it is best to dry-clean it, although you can machine-wash and iron the cloth while it is still damp. Never bleach linen.

As unique souvenirs of Krakow, linen tablecloths are a particularly good buy. They come in many styles, from traditional folk designs to the ultra-modern. Many are richly hand-embroidered, either in bright colours or in subtle matching thread. Folk embroidery peasant blouses and dresses are also available.

The more traditional designs in linenwear are easily found inside the Sukiennice and other craft shops mostly around Rynek Główny. Modern designs can be found in the boutiques on Floriańska and Grodzka. One of the best shops for raw linen cloth is next to the Ethnographic Museum at *Plac Wolnica 2* (*tel: (012) 430 6124*). In the museum itself you can view examples of traditional folk technology used to harvest, pound and press flax as well as the final cloth products (*see pp100–01*).

Opposite top: Linen cloth for sale
Opposite bottom: Dried flax
Above: Cracovian natives in traditional linen costumes

Entertainment

The art scene is the very soul of Krakow. There are galleries on every street of Old Town and Kazimierz and less formal exhibits are common in bars, restaurants and hotels. Live bands play at many venues and buskers from all over Central Europe play on the streets.

Krakow's many galleries cater to every taste

ART GALLERIES
Galleries are particularly thick on the ground in Old Town and Kazimierz. Those listed below are just a small selection.

Krypta u Pijarów
A beautiful space in the crypts of the Piarist church at the end of ul. Jana. Run by a Roman Catholic culture association, the exhibits often have religious themes.
ul. Pijarska 2. Tel: (012) 430 2015.

Olympia
A small gallery in Kazimierz with a personal touch. The art is often unlabelled and discussion with the staff is encouraged.
ul. Estery 16. Tel: (012) 429 3734. Open: Tue–Sat, 11am–7pm.

Space Gallery
An astounding space on ul. Floriańska. The walls are covered in 17th-century frescoes and the floor is crowded with antiques and the cream of the crop of early 20th-century Krakow art.
ul. Floriańska 13. Tel: (012) 432 2920. Open: Mon–Fri 10am–6.30pm, Sat 10am–3pm.

Starmach
This gallery occupies the building of a majestic old prayer-house in the less-famous Jewish district of Podgórze. The art concentrates on Kantor and his successors in the Krakow Group.
ul. Węgierska 5. Tel: (012) 656 4317. Open: Mon–Fri 11am–6pm.

CINEMA
Krakow's tradition of small, arty urban cinemas is slowly giving way to vast multiplexes on the outskirts of town. In spite of a number of critical successes in local Polish film-making, the repertoire of films in Krakow is also shifting towards the sort of Hollywood blockbusters that can fill the multiplexes. Most films are shown in the original language with subtitles. Only films for children are dubbed.

The best source for showing times is the *Co Jest Grane* section of Friday's *Gazeta Wyborcza*. Several internet portals carry the week's listings.

MUSIC
Cracovians are dedicated fans of all varieties of music. Outside formal concert halls, there are also many occasional concerts in churches, museums and university halls. June is

particularly crowded with music festivals. Keep an eye open for posters or ask at the Cultural Information Centre for more details on *ul. Jana 2 (tel: (012) 421 7787)*.

Concert Halls
Filharmonia
The Philharmonic is one of Krakow's most highly regarded cultural treasures. It is regularly visited by world-class composers, conductors and soloists.
ul. Zwierzyniecka 1. Tel: (012) 429 1438. www.filharmonia.krakow.pl. Most concerts start at 6pm or 7.30pm.

Folk Music
In Krakow, the folk music scene is dominated by folk-themed restaurants. All of the following have regular concerts of live folk music: Morskie Oko, Chłopskie Jadło, Alef, Ariel and Smak Ukraiński. Zakopane (*see p139*) is also a major centre for the commercialisation of all kinds of folk culture.

Jazz
'Hot' jazz made an impact on Krakow before the Second World War. Under communism Krakow still managed to produce jazzmen of European renown such as Tomas Stańko (*b.* 1942). There are now several jazz bars in Krakow, a few of which are listed below.

Harris Piano Jazz Bar
It is hard to get a seat with a view in this cellar on the main square but the music sounds all right. Mostly younger bands.
Rynek Główny 28. Tel: (012) 421 5741. Open: daily 10pm–2am.

Indigo
Somewhat irregular jazz concerts with a decidedly eclectic taste but local jazz enthusiasts proclaim this the best musical venue in the city. On non-concert weekends the crowd gets younger and the music tends towards danceable acid jazz, hip-hop and funk.
ul. Floriańska 26. Tel: (012) 429 1743. Open: daily 3pm–3am.

Kornet
This dark, low-ceilinged, underground club near the Błonia magically transforms into Krakow's most intimate Dixieland & blues jazz experience under the influence of Wednesday night's jam-concert. Local and visiting musicians often jump in on rambling improvisations on jazz standards.
Al. Krasińskiego 19. Tel: (012) 427 0244. Open: daily 11am–midnight.

U Muniaka
In 1992, trumpeter Janusz Muniak (*b.* 1941) opened one of the first jazz bars in Old Town. These days, the concerts on Thursday, Friday and Saturday have fallen into a rut but still make an enjoyable night out.
ul. Floriańska 3. Tel: (012) 423 1205. Open: daily 6.30pm–2am.

Opera and Operetta
Although Krakow has excellent theatre and an excellent orchestra, somehow it has never developed much of an opera company. The Krakow Opera plays on two smallish stages, so check which it is using for the performance that you wish to see.
Scena Operetkowa: ul. Lubicz 48.

Tel: (012) 421 4200. Scena Operowa,
Teatr Słowackiego: pl. św. Ducha.
Tel: (012) 421 1630.
www.opera.krakow.pl

NIGHTLIFE

Krakow's nightlife is built around the
assumption that clients will walk in off
the street without any special advertise-
ment. A copy of the bimonthly *In Your
Pocket* will help you find the hidden
treasures but visitors have to keep an eye
open for posters for special parties or DJs.

Any concentration of drunk or
distracted tourists will attract a certain
amount of crime. Do not leave handbags
unattended at your table if you go to
dance, buy drinks, etc.

As a university town, dress codes are
usually relaxed in Krakow, although
many locals dress up quite elegantly
to go out on the town. Some clubs
may refuse clients in trainers or track
suits.

Cabaret, Floor Shows

Krakow has a long tradition of cabarets,
going back to the first true cabaret in
Poland, *Zielony Balonik* (*The Green
Balloon*) in 1905. Visitors are warned
that Krakow cabaret can be very
self-referential and involve obscure
political jokes.

Loch Camelot

ul. św. Tomasza 17. Tel: (012) 423 0638.
www.lochcamelot.art.pl. Performances:
Fri 8.15pm and other times as posted.

Piwnica Pod Baranami

Rynek Główny 25. Tel: (012) 421 2500.
Performances: Sat 9pm.

Casinos (Kasyno)

Most casinos in Poland are in hotels.
You must be able to show a valid
passport in order to enter a casino.
All winnings are tax-free.

Casinos Poland – Kasyno w Hotelu Novotel Bronowice

*ul. Armii Krajowej 11. Tel: (012) 636
0807. www.casinospoland.pl. Open:
daily 11am–2am. Buses: 139, 159, 173.*

Orbis Casino

The casino is located within the Sofitel
Hotel. *ul. Konopnickiej 28. Tel: (012)
267 6610. Open: daily 1pm–5am. Buses:
164, 173, 179.*

Salon Gier – PTTK

Smaller than the others, with lower
minimum bets and better odds.
*ul. Westerplatte 15/16. Tel: (012) 422
9500 ext. 541.*

Dancing

Warsaw and Łódź are more famous for
their dance and club scenes than Krakow
but occasionally one of the star DJs will
travel south. Keep a lookout for posters.

Roentgen

Much too small to dance in, but that
does not stop anyone. Light house, trance,
acid jazz. The bouncers may demand a
'membership card' but explain that you
are visitors in town. *pl. Szczepański 3.
Tel: (012) 431 1177. www.roentgen.pl.
Open: daily 4pm–4am.*

Strefa 22

A comfortable set of apartments
overlooking the main square. The local

DJs favour techno but imported DJs enlighten the crowd with drum'n'bass and acid jazz. Young crowd. *Rynek Główny 22. Tel: (012) 292 5532. Open: Sun–Thur 1pm–midnight, Fri–Sat 1pm–3am.*

Szara

Hot-blooded dancers set the dance floor on fire with Latino ballroom dance when this restaurant turns into a club late on weekend nights. *Rynek Główny 6. Tel: (012) 421 6669. www.szara.pl. Open: daily 8am–11pm.*

Student Clubs

Krakow's nightlife is dominated by the student population. However, there are also special 'student clubs' that allow entrance only with a valid student ID or charge non-students higher cover charges. Most student clubs play a mix of rock classics and current hits. The beer is always cheap and the clientele is young and open to meeting strangers.

Pod Jaszczurami

The toughest door policy on Rynek Główny: no valid student ID, no entrance. Fidel Castro once used the toilets. Very much in demand on weekend nights. *Rynek Główny 8. Tel: (012) 429 4538. Open: daily 10am–4am.*

Pub Studencki DNS

Known universally as 'Świniarnia' (the Swinery), a big underground hall filled with billiards, darts, air hockey, internet connections, cheap beer, smoke and very loud music. *ul. Budryka 6. Tel: (012) 636 0441. Open: daily 10am–2am. Buses: 139, 159, 173.*

Rotunda

Films, concerts, lectures and weekend-night (start at 8pm) rock dance parties. *ul. Oleandry 1. Tel: (012) 633 3538. Open: daily 8pm–2am. Trams: 15, 18.*

THEATRE

Krakow is famous throughout Central Europe for its high standards in theatre. Unfortunately, for most visitors the language barrier will bar them from full enjoyment of this aspect of Krakow life.

Bagatela

Specialising in comedy and lighter shows, Bagatela often performs foreign works in translation, some of which may be familiar enough for visitors to follow. *ul. Karmelicka 6. Tel: (012) 292 7219. Most shows begin at 7.15pm.*

Słowacki

A very fancy and very yellow theatre just off of ul. Szpitalna. The repertoire, including Shakespeare and Opera, is top class as is the décor of this theatre. *pl. św. Ducha 1. Tel: (012) 423 1700 (booking). Most shows begin at 7pm.*

Stary

This is Krakow's most sacred shrine to Melpomene where an endless parade of great Polish actors and actresses got their start (before moving to Warsaw). The repertoire and staging of works here is devoted to the sometimes obscure and hermetic Cracovian theatre tradition. *ul. Jagiellonska 5. Tel: (012) 421 2977, 421 8848. Show times vary considerably depending on the length of the work.*

Children

Children may find a heavy diet of churches and museums a bit hard to digest but there are many attractions in Krakow intended for younger palates. The cheap and safe public transport encourages many older children to explore the city on their own.

Non-sheep-eating dragons!

A ride around Old Town in a horse-drawn carriage is a good place to start with children, especially if the driver lets them try their hand at the reins. Afterwards, you can feed the pigeons on Rynek Główny: this brings a squeal of delight to children of all ages. A trip to Wieliczka Salt Mines will enthral older children but younger ones might prefer the much shorter (and spookier) Dragon's Den. The collection of medieval weapons in the Wawel Armoury will satisfy any budding knights in your family and a cruise up the river to Bielany on the Wisła ferry will shiver the timbers of your pirates.

Art Centre

Pracownia Twórczości Artystycznej Dzieci i Młodzieży (Creative Artistic Workshop for Children and Youth) is an old synagogue on ul. Szeroka that has been converted into an art centre for local children. Mornings are usually dedicated to ongoing classes but on Tuesday, Wednesday and Friday at about 3.30pm there are open activities that visitors may attend. It might turn out to be just the place to drop off children who would not enjoy a walking tour of Kazimierz. Call ahead to see what the day's activities will be and whether it will be accessible to non-Polish-speaking children.
ul. Szeroka 16. Tel: (012) 421 2987. Open: daily 9am–7pm.

Cinema

Unfortunately for visiting children, films aimed at younger audiences are always dubbed into Polish. Parents with toddlers, however, will appreciate Multikino (*ul. Dobrego Pasterza 128; tel: (012) 617 6399*) and its special Wednesday morning showings of films for *parents* with small children. The ticket price includes an extra seat for those hampers of nappies and talcum powder. The soundtrack is set quieter than usual and the room temperature is higher. Even if your baby starts bawling in the middle of the film, no-one will ask you to leave.

Classical Music

Opera Krakowska (*ul. Lubicz 27; tel: (012) 628 9113*) has matinée showings (usually 11am) of opera for children, which tends to fill up with school groups. Filharmonia (*ul. Zwierzyniecka 1; tel: (012) 429 1438*) also has a similar series *Koncerty dla dzieci* (concerts for children).

Go-Karting
Motodrom Gokartowy (Go-Kart Motodrome)

Children seven years old and up (or at least tall enough to reach the pedals) can zip around a tyre-lined course while their parents admire the beautiful old Kazimierz tram shed it is housed in.
ul. św. Wawrzyńca 12. Tel: (0601) 48 67 90. Open: daily noon–11pm.

Park Jordana (Jordan's Park)

A big park packed with things for youngsters to do. The renowned Professor Jordan of the Jagiellonian University felt that children needed to exercise both mind and body, leading to this interesting mix of outdoor museum (busts of great Polish writers) and sports field (basketball courts, a small kayaking pond, etc.) in part financed by Jordan himself. More recent additions include a skateboarding ramp. It is best in summer but even in winter there are places for sledding.
Between ul. Reymonta and Al. 3 Maja. Trams: 15, 18. Free admission.

Puppet Theatre
Podgórski Teatr Lalki

Traditional puppet theatre for younger children.
ul. Zamoyskiego 50. Tel: (012) 656 1050. Trams: 8, 10, 11, 23.

Teatr Groteska

A 'puppet' theatre that boisterously pushes far beyond the boundaries of traditional puppetry with masks, giant puppets, puppets that transform from one thing into another and shows where puppets share the stage with live actors. The stories draw on everything from Homer to Ursula LeGuin. Plays are in Polish but some stories may be familiar enough to follow. Times and prices vary.
ul. Skarbowa 2. Tel: (012) 633 9604, reservations 633 3762. Buses: 164, 173, 179.

Water Park
Park Wodny

Water slides, a 'wild river', climbing walls, fountains, youngsters' pool, video games and fast food. Children under three enter for free, under seven at reduced rates. Lifeguards on duty. Jacuzzi, hydro-massage, sauna and tanning booth for parents, too.
ul. Dobrego Pasterza 126. Tel: (012) 616 3190. www.parkwodny.pl. Buses: 128, 129, 198.

Zoo
(see pp143–4)

A resident of the Zoo in Las Wolski

Sport and Leisure

Krakow's Bractwo Kurkowe (the Brotherhood of the Rooster) was already in existence by the end of the 13th century, easily qualifying it as the oldest sporting club in town. To this day, its members practise their shooting skills in preparation for their annual tournament at Corpus Christi when the winner is declared the Rooster King for the year. Their name comes from the wooden rooster that they use as a target.

Fishing on the banks of the Vistula

Billiards

A fairly common bar-room sport in Poland these days. You will find individual tables all over Old Town, such as the two in Music Club Frantic (*ul. Szewska 5*). Pub Studencki DNS (*ul. Budryka 6*) out in the Student Town has a whole hall full of them.

Bowling
Fantasy Park

Al. Pokoju 44. Tel: (012) 290 9515. www.fantasypark.pl. Open: Mon–Fri noon–midnight, Sat–Sun noon–1am. Trams: 1, 7, 14, 15, 22.

Fencing
Krakowski Klub Szermierzy

With a glorious history that goes back to the days when gentlemen at the Jagiellonian University had Fencing as a subject with its own professor. Contact the club for information on lessons and how to book.

ul. Tadeusza Kościuszki 24 (around the back of the building). Tel/fax: (012) 422 7058. www.kks.krakow.pl. Trams: 1, 2, 6.

Fitness Centres
Euro Fitness Club

Aerobics, yoga, power step, weight room, sauna, massage, beautician.

ul. Sówackiego 64. Tel: (012) 634 2000. www.efc.pl/ang/index.htm

Fitness Klub Pi

Aerobics, weight room, sauna, massage, tanning booth.

ul. Koło Strzelnicy 5. Tel/fax: (012) 425 3850. www.fitness-pi.com.pl

Football (soccer)

The mighty rivalry between Krakow's two top clubs, Wisła and Cracovia, has produced some great football. However, it also produces a lot of hooligans. Matches are closely guarded by legions of police in riot gear, and men under the age of 30 must have special ID cards in order to get into the stadium. Visit the stadium where the match will be played between 9am and 3pm to get your ID for a small sum (bring a photograph). Cracovia's colours are red and white; Wisła's are blue, red and white.

Krakow's fencing tradition is alive and well

Cracovia
ul. Kałuży 1. Tel: (012) 427 3562.
www.cracovia.krakow.pl
Wisła
ul. Reymonta 22. Tel: (012) 630 7602.
www.wisla.krakow.pl

Golf
Krakow Valley Golf and Country Club
Paczółtowice. Tel: (012) 282 9467.
www.krakow-valley.com
Royal Kraków Golf and Country Club
Ochmanów 124, Podłęże. Tel: (012) 281 9171. www.krakowgolf.pl

Squash
Botoja Squash Centre
ul. Jósefa 14. Tel: (012) 421 5187.
www.botoja.pl. Open: 2–10pm except Sat & Sun noon–10pm.
Gołaski Sport
Seven tennis courts (all are covered in winter), four squash courts and a gym out in Wola Justowska.
ul. Królowej Jadwigi 220. Tel: (012) 425 3900. www.golaskisport.com.pl

Swimming
Blocks of swimming time are often reserved by groups. You will have a better chance of finding space when schools are not in session.
Akademia Ekonomiczna – Studium Wychowania Fizycznego i Sportu
ul. Rakowicka 27. Tel/fax: (012) 293 5070.
Kryta Pływalnia Akademii Pedagogicznej
ul. Ingardena 4 (entrance from ul. Oleandry). Tel: (012) 634 2625.

Tennis
Gółaski Sport
(*see* Squash, *above*)
Klub Sportowy Grzegórzecki
Six tennis courts, two of which are covered in winter.
Al. Pokoju 16. Tel: (012) 411 6149.
Klub Sportowy Zwierzyniecki
Six tennis courts, two of which can be used in winter, sport shop.
ul. Na Błonia 1. Tel: (012) 425 1846.

Bowling is new, but growing in popularity

Food and Drink

Lard. In Poland, it is not just a shortening. It is a condiment, a major ingredient and sometimes it is served up at your table with bread as food in and of itself.

The basic ingredient of Polish cuisine is pork. Vegetarians beware!

Polish food is very Central European. It is notable for its heavy emphasis on a short list of ingredients: pork, potatoes and cabbage. While visitors to Poland are usually impressed at the skill with which those basic ingredients can be manipulated into new shapes, they may grow weary of them by the end of their sojourn.

Vegetarians will be frustrated to find that the Polish concept of *danie jarskie* (sometimes mistranslated as 'vegetarian meal') really means something like 'a meal wherein meat isn't the single largest ingredient'. Nearly every food is kissed by lard or meat-based stock at some point in its production. A handful of vegetarian restaurants offer the only respite.

Polish bread (*chleb*) is worth singling out for special praise. Bought fresh from the baker, it is a self-contained feast. A local variant found almost exclusively on the streets of Krakow is the *obwarzanek*, a relative of the bagel. This round circle of chewy bread is often dusted with salt, poppy seeds or sesame seeds. It often stands in for a more substantial breakfast for Cracovians who are short of time in the morning.

Starters (przystawki)
rydze smażone fried orange agaric mushrooms

śledź w śmietanie herring in cream with onions

Soups (zupy)
barszcz beetroot soup
barszcz ukraiński beetroot soup blanched with cream
chłodnik cold beetroot soup
grzybowa wild mushroom soup
jarzynowa vegetable soup
krupnik barley soup
ogórkowa pickle soup
pomidorowa tomato soup
rosół broth/bouillon
żurek fermented rye soup

Main Dishes
bigos hunter's cabbage and meat stew
fasolka po bretońsku heavy bean stew
flaki (flaczki) tripe
gołąbki meat and rice wrapped in cabbage
golonka pig's trotters served with the skin (and sometimes a bit of hair) still on it
gulasz węgierski Hungarian goulash
kaczka pieczona z jabłkami roast duck with apple
karp po żydowsku Jewish-style carp
kaszanka black pudding
kiełbasa sausage (there are hundreds of different kinds)
kotlet de volaille chicken Kiev
kotlet schabowy wiener schnitzel
pieczeń z dzika roast wild boar

pstrąg z grilla grilled trout
schab faszerowany z śliwkami pork stuffed with prunes
wątróbka liver
zrazy wołowe beef roll-ups

Dumplings
kopytka solid dumpling of flour and potato
pierogi ruskie ravioli filled with a mixture of potatoes and cheese
pierogi z kapustą i grzybami ravioli filled with cabbage and wild mushroom
pierogi z mięsem ravioli filled with minced meat
pierogi z serem ravioli filled with sweet cheese

Vegetables
buraki beetroot
cebula onion
frytki chips (French fries)
kapusta cabbage
kapusta kiszona sauerkraut
kasza groats
marchewka carrot
ogórki cucumber/pickle
placki ziemniaczane potato pancakes
pomidory tomatoes
ziemniaki potatoes

Dessert
makowiec poppy-seed cake
naleśniki z serem crêpes with sweet cheese
pączki jam doughnuts
piernik gingerbread
sernik cheesecake
szarlotka apple pie

Cheese
bryndza aged soft white sheep's cheese

bundz unaged semi-soft white sheep's cheese
oscypek aged hard sheep's cheese (usually smoked)
ser wiejski cottage cheese
ser żółty hard yellow cheese
twaróg semi-soft white cows' cheese

Where to Eat
The bewitching atmosphere of Old Town is a spice for every dish. The cellars and state rooms of the old palaces and *kamienice* have been expertly renovated as elegant restaurants and Krakow's cosmopolitan appreciation of good food and drink remains undamaged by the years of communism.

Unfortunately, service is often Krakow's weakest point. Staff can be

Pork and potatoes, ingredients of a typical Polish dish

slow and indifferent to customer needs. If you receive good service at any of Krakow's restaurants, be sure to encourage such behaviour in the future by tipping. The usual amount is 10 per cent, although for smaller sums (such as two coffees without a meal) leaving the change is more common. If your bill is, for example, zł8.50 and you wish the waitress to keep the change from a zł10 note, simply say 'dziękuję' (thank you) when handing her the money.

Most restaurants are clearly marked as such. A few straddle the boundary between restaurants and cafés. Bars and pubs rarely have much more than crisps and pretzels to eat. Restaurants are thick enough on the ground in Old Town that you can wander around from locale to locale to see what takes your fancy. Alternatively, the listings in the bimonthly *Krakow in Your Pocket* are a good source of ideas.

Milk Bars

One of the great joys of Krakow are the many cheap and cheerful *bar mleczny* (milk bars) that serve up mighty portions of hearty home cooking at prices that even feckless students and undiscovered artists can afford. They are not usually open for supper but they make a great lunch break when sightseeing. *Bar mleczny* usually serve a few almost-vegetarian dishes (no actual pieces of meat, but will usually contain lard or meat-based stock) and are always strictly self-service.

Pod Temidą

Simple but satisfying. On a well-beaten tourist track, mostly patronised by students from nearby university buildings.
ul. Grodzka 43.
Tel: (012) 422 0874.

Różowy Słoń (Pink Elephant)

This milk bar's trademark brightly-painted pop-art walls make reference to everything from Barbie dolls to Batman. Recently, they have expanded to become a sort of home-grown fast-food chain.
ul. Sienna 3.
Tel: (012) 421 8322.
ul. Straszewskiego 24.
Tel: (012) 423 0757.

U Pani Stasi (At Mrs Stanislava's Place)

A Krakow landmark.

Crowded and slightly chaotic it is best navigated with a Polish friend.
ul. Mikołajska 16.
Tel: (012) 421 5084.

Restaurants

In addition to Krakow's eateries for students and artists, an increasing number of world-class restaurants have opened for more refined tastes. The assortment ranges from hearty Central European meat and potatoes to exotic dishes from every corner of the world.

Restaurant prices in Krakow have remained relatively affordable in spite of a rapid change in the market. Restaurants near tourist sites are often, but not always, slightly more expensive than elsewhere. Although subject to change, the following guide to prices will give an indication of relative costs. Average meal prices are given in złoty and are inclusive of beer or table wine for a two-course meal for two people.

★ up to zł119
★★ zł120 to 179
★★★ zł180 to 239
★★★★ zł240 or above

A meal out

French
A la Carte ★★★★
Perfectly-prepared dishes served in dainty portions down in Kazimierz. French with Oriental and Caribbean influences. Faultless service in a well-lit, modern space.
ul. Izaaka 7. Tel: (012) 430 6550; e-mail: restauracja@alacarte.pl. Open: daily 11am–last guest.

Cyrano de Bergerac ★★★★
Comfortable bourgeois grace in a spacious Old Town cellar. The menu and wine list are more French than the French.
ul. Sławkowska 26. Tel: (012) 411 7288.

www.cyranodebergerac.pl. Open: Mon–Sat noon–midnight.

La Fontaine ★★
A more relaxed atmosphere than most of Krakow's French restaurants. Excellent desserts, including crème brûlée. The cellar decor includes the titular fountain.
ul. Sławkowska 1. Tel: (012) 431 0955. Open: daily noon–midnight.

International
CK Browar ★★
This underground restaurant/beer hall is most famous for its microbrew produced on the premises, CK Browar also serves up delicious meals from across the old Austro-Hungarian Empire. The noisy beer hall is in front of you as you enter. The quieter restaurant is to the left.
ul. Podwale 6/7 (on the corner, downstairs). Tel: (012) 429 2505 ext 107. Open: daily noon–midnight.

Copernicus ★★★★
Sophisticated continental cuisine with Polish accents in a daringly-renovated, spacious old *kamienica*. Everything is done with flair and

aplomb. Excellent service and a top-notch wine list.
ul. Kanonicza 16. Tel: (012) 424 3421. Open: daily noon–11pm.

Metropolitan ★★
International fusion cuisine in an open and airy space with generous tables. Great cocktails and salads. Generous US- and UK-style breakfasts. Perfect for business lunches.
ul. Sławkowska 3. Tel: (012) 421 9803. Open: daily 7am–midnight (last order at 11pm).

Szara ★★
Arty and traditional at the same time. Historic neo-Gothic interiors remade as chic bars and booths. One of the few restaurants in Krakow to make a serious commitment to seafood.
Rynek Główny 6. Tel: (012) 421 6669. Open: daily 8am–11pm.

Italian
Avanti ★★
Pseudo-Roman interiors in a cellar just outside Old Town. The pasta is both excellent and cheap.
ul. Karmelicka 7. Tel: (012) 430 0770. Open: daily noon–midnight.

There are restaurants in some very beautiful settings

Da Pietro ★
Hearty Italian food served in liberal portions. Succulent sauces. In the summer, the outdoor garden on the Rynek offers starlit dining.
Rynek Główny 17. Tel: (012) 422 3279. Open: daily 12.30pm–midnight.

Jewish
Alef ★★
Home-like atmosphere with mismatched antiques and a wandering cat. Jewish-style meals (not strictly kosher), good coffee and excellent charoset (chopped apples, nuts and cinnamon).

ul. Szeroka 17. Tel: (012) 421 3870. Open: daily 9am–10pm.

Eden ★★
The only strictly kosher restaurant in Krakow, inside the Eden Hotel. You cannot just walk in off the street and expect to be served immediately. All their (pre-packaged) meals must be requested at least three hours in advance. A telephone call is sufficient or meals can be ordered online up to a year in advance.
ul. Ciemna 15. Tel: (012) 430 6565.
www.hoteleden.pl. Open: Sun–Fri lunch and dinner, Sat lunch only.

Klezmer Hois ★★
Housed in the old *mikveh* (Jewish ritual baths), whose columns are still visible, a quiet and comfortable café-restaurant run by the same people as Alef. Jewish-style, not strictly kosher.
ul. Szeroka 6. Tel: (012) 411 1245. Open: daily 9am–10pm.

Polish
Chłopskie Jadło ★★
Live folk music after 10pm. Huge portions of Polish folk cuisine, usually pork. The *barszcz* (beetroot soup) with

dumplings is outstanding and the *niecka* (literally: a trough) is a huge sampler of nearly everything on the menu for groups. Pseudo-village barnyard folk decoration.
ul. św. Jana 3. Tel: (012) 421 8520, 429 5157. Open: Sun–Fri noon–10pm, Sat noon–midnight.

Morskie Oko ★★
Vigorous live folk music. Zakopane-style wooden folk decoration with a central staircase hewn from a giant tree trunk. The *kwaśnica* is a highlander's sour cabbage soup.
pl. Szczepański 8. Tel: (012) 431 2423, 431 2472. Open: daily noon–midnight.

Ogniem i Mieczem ★★
Off the beaten track, named after Henryk Sienkiewicz's romance about the 1648 Cossack rebellion. Cannon in the garden and hussar's armour by the door. Dishes based on historical recipes and a selection of meads (wine made from honey).
pl. Serkowskiego 7. Tel: (012) 656 2328. Open: Mon–Sat noon–midnight, Sun noon–10pm.

Pod Aniołami ★★
Food based on the aristocratic tradition in Polish cuisine in a deep Gothic cellar full of antiques. Lots of beech-wood grilled meats, especially game, and salads.
ul. Grodzka 35. Tel: (012) 421 3999. Open: daily 1pm–midnight except Fri & Sat 1pm–1am.

Soplicowo ★★★
Centrally located. Traditional Polish foods with a subtle modern twist. The often under-rated food of *kasza* (groats) is presented in a whole selection of types and styles. Tall ceilings and 19th-century bric-à-brac.
Rynek Główny 22. Tel: (012) 431 0880. Open: daily 10am–2am. Rynek Główny 15. Tel: (012) 292 1088, 422 1035, 422 1296. Open: daily noon–midnight.

Tetmajerowska ★★★★
Upstairs from Hawełka, genteel and cultured dining in rooms decorated by one of Krakow's most famous early 20th-century artists. A traditional Polish menu without surprises but the starters, especially the caviar and the herrings in cream, are classics.
Rynek Główny 34 (upstairs). Tel: (012) 422 0631, 422 4753, 422 5864. Open: daily 12.30–11.30pm. Closed: Monday.

Wierzynek ★★★
A very opulent restaurant crammed with antiques and artwork. Aristocratic Polish cuisine with a

Bright colours and cheap food at Różowy Słoń

French influence. You cannot go wrong with the duck. The date over the door, 1364, refers to a famous feast of kings and princes that later tradition ascribed to Mikołaj Wierzynek, who once owned a building that might have been on the site of the current restaurant.
Rynek Główny 15.
Tel: (012) 424 9600.
Open: 1pm–midnight.

Vegetarian
Green Way ★
A self-service, no-frills little eatery with medieval setting in the heart of Old Town. Very few tables so you may have to share.
ul. Mikołajska 12.
Tel: (012) 431 1027.
Open: Mon–Fri 10am–10pm, Sat–Sun 11am–9pm.

Momo ★
Rich, spicy food with an Indian-Tibetan accent near Kazimierz. Wonderful hot bean soup and spiced coffee.
ul. Dietla 49. Tel: (0609) 68 57 75. Open: daily 11am–8pm.

Vega ★
Two quiet locations with home-style furnishings. Lots of salads, casseroles and tofu-patty creations.
ul. św. Gertrudy 7.
Tel: (012) 422 3494.
ul. Krupnicza 22.
Open: daily 9am–9pm.

What to Drink
Beer (*Piwo*)
Most Polish beers are fairly heavy Pilsner-type lagers. A few major brands dominate the market, of which, **Żywiec**, **Okocim** and **Tyskie** are most common around Krakow. Smaller brands with strictly local distribution are common in the smaller towns. Żywiec also produces a heavier, dark caramel porter (stout) that many consider to be the best of its kind.

Beer is usually served colder than room temperature in Poland. However, in winter many bars serve up *piwo grzane* (hot mulled beer) with cloves, cinnamon and fruit syrup. The last ingredient is sometimes added to cold beer in the warmer months as well as *piwo z sokiem.*

Mead (*Miód Pitny*)
Poland is one of the few countries still producing much of this ancient drink. Mead is fermented honey. In Poland, meads are ranked according to the proportions of water to honey. **Półtorak** is two parts honey to one part water; **dwójniak** is one to one; **trójniak** is one to two; **czwórniak** is one part honey to three parts water. Półtorak is usually a heavy, sweet dessert drink whereas high-quality dwójniak or trójniak will go well with supper. Some meads will have herbs, spices or fruit juice added.

Microbrew ginger beer at C K Browar

New bars appear all the time

Vodka (*Wódka*)

Clear vodka (*czysta*) is the colourless spirit that most people associate with the word. However, Poland produces a rich selection of flavoured vodkas as well (*see pp170–1*). Vodka is usually drunk in neat shots, not in cocktails. It is sometimes followed by a non-alcoholic chaser like orange juice. You do not need to drain your entire glass of vodka in a single go.

Wine (*Wino*)

Poland doesn't produce its own wine commercially. Most restaurants and some bars will have a fairly international wine list but the best bargains are from other Central and Eastern European countries like Hungary and Bulgaria. Wines from France and Italy are routinely overpriced for their quality.

Where to Drink

Krakow's hundreds of bars and pubs are a tourist attraction that bring in crowds of visitors from Warsaw and other Polish towns every weekend. New places open up every month. There is no reason to limit yourself to the list that follows:

Above Ground in Old Town

Camelot

Folksy, painted-wood interiors. There is a popular cabaret downstairs in the evenings and the garden outside in Doubting Thomas's Nook is a beloved summertime gathering point. Salads and light meals available. *ul. św. Tomasza 17.*

Tel: (012) 421 0123. Open: daily 9am–midnight.

Le Fumoir

Plush modernist interiors, live piano music, cigars and a decent selection of brandies and single malts. *ul. Sławkowska 26. Tel: (012) 411 7288. Open: 7pm–1am. Closed: Sun.*

Paparazzi

Slick and stylish bar for actors, models, expatriate businessmen and Scandinavian medical students, decorated with black and white photographs. A cosmopolitan selection of cocktails and imported alcohol as well as a menu of light food. *ul. Mikołajska 9. Tel: (012) 429 4597. Open: Mon–Fri 11am–1am, Sat–Sun 4pm 1am.*

Stalowe Magnolie

Rich fabrics and fantastic, organic-looking lighting. The back-room bar has a huge row of four-poster beds to lounge on. If you do not have a membership card, you can get in by looking the part and pressing the buzzer by the door.

Live music with a rock and blues emphasis on weekend nights (usually starts at 9pm).

The summer garden at Camelot is a good place to see and be seen

ul. św. Jana 15. Tel: (012) 422 6084. Open: daily 6pm–last guest.

Kazimierz Knajpy

Alchemia
A dark and magical lair in which to sample mysterious potions. Some rooms can be reached only by walking through a wardrobe. The entrance is from Plac Nowy, the nucleus of an increasingly popular nightlife district away from Old Town.
ul. Estery 5. Tel: (012) 421 2200; www. alchemia.com.pl. Open: Mon–Sat 11am–4am, Sun 10am–4am.

Alef
(*see* Jewish restaurants *p164*)

Les Couleurs Café
A little bit of France in Kazimierz. Pastis, espresso, French wine, quiche and pastries. Jacques Brel and Serge Gainsbourg on the stereo.
ul. Estery 10. Tel: (012) 429 4270. Open: daily 7am–2am except Sat 8am–2am, Sun 9am–2am.

Singer
Candle-lit tables made from Singer sewing machines and melancholy French jazz playing on the stereo.
*ul. Estery 20.
Tel: (012) 292 0622.
Open: daily 9am–3am.*

Warsztat Café
A music-themed pub with frequent live performances.
ul. Izaaka 3.

*Tel: (012) 421 4865.
Open: daily 10am–2am.*

Old Town Cafés

Europejska
A cosmopolitan pub-café where men in serious suits drink coffee in little cups. Plush booths and an inexplicable London telephone kiosk. Dessert comes in many tempting variations: try the hot *szarlotka* with ice cream.
*Rynek Główny 35. Tel: (012) 429 3493. www. europejska.krakow.pl.
Open: daily 8am–midnight.*

Jama Michalika
As much a museum as a café, do not leave Krakow without visiting this shrine to the Young Poland movement. The slow-moving staff will give you plenty of time to admire the stained glass and bizarre furniture.
*ul. Floriańska 45.
Tel: (012) 422 1561.
www.jamamichalika.pl.
Open: daily 9am–10pm.*

Noworolski
A bastion of immutable Cracoviana in the Sukiennice. The decor remains essentially the same as it was when Krakow was part of the Austro-Hungarian Empire. Delicious coffee and cakes are served to

the Old Guard among cigarette smoke and philosophical conversation. Good breakfast options.
Rynek Główny 1. Tel: (012) 422 4771. Open: daily 9am–last guest.

Pożegnanie z Afryką (Out of Africa)
Coffee, lots of different kinds of coffee and nothing but coffee. They do not serve tea or any kind of alcohol.
ul. św. Tomasza 21 (there is also an entrance from ul. Floriańska 15). Tel/fax: (012) 632 8945. Open: daily 10am–10.15pm.

Old Town Cellars (*piwnice*)
Faust
A large and boisterous underground labyrinth that caters to Krakow's many students. On weekend nights it gets even louder with dance parties.
Rynek Główny 6. Tel: (012) 431 1004. Open: daily noon the party ends.

Klub Indigo
A mellower cellar-bar than most and the music leans towards jazz.
ul. Floriańska 26. Tel: (012) 421 4865. Open: Sun–Thur

4pm–midnight, Fri–Sat 4pm–2am.

Molière
This upmarket bar may have the only wheelchair-accessible *piwnica* in all of Krakow.
ul. Szewska 4. Tel: (012) 292 6400. Open: Mon–Sat 9am–2am, Sun 10am–2am.

U Louisa
A classic on Krakow's nightlife scene and one of the first internet cafés in town.
Rynek Główny 13. Tel: (012) 617 0222. Open: daily 11am–1am.

Late-night alchemy at Alchemia

As Somerset Maugham wrote of Poland's celebrated Żubrówka, 'It smells of freshly mown hay and spring flowers, of thyme and lavender, and it's soft on the palate and so comfortable, it's like listening to music by moonlight.'

Although most people elsewhere associate the word 'vodka' with clear, colourless spirits, Poland produces over 300 varieties of *wódka*, many of which are flavoured. Short-term visitors to Poland may not have

time to sample them all, but they are an experience not to be missed. Many of Poland's finest vodkas are unavailable in other countries.

The starting point of every vodka is a natural spirit. Most spirits produced in Poland are distilled from grain or potato mash. Clear varieties of vodka contain nothing else. A small quantity of spirits is distilled from fruit, such as the throat-scorching *śliwowica* (plum schnapps) or milder *winiak* (grape brandy).

The more common approach is to soak fruit in a grain vodka until the alcohol takes on colour and flavour. Almost any fruit can be treated this way but thick and sweet *wiśniówka* (cherry cordial) is an often-served dessert drink at holiday meals. The flavour is deceptively mild: most varieties of *wiśniówka* are 50 per cent alcohol.

Another vodka for your sweet tooth is *krupnik*, a liqueur made by mixing honey and a bouquet of herbs and spices into vodka. Up to the 19th century, hot *krupnik* was served with melted butter to warm the innards of frozen travellers in the winter. No-one serves it with butter any more, but you can still find a few bars in Krakow that will serve *krupnik* hot with a slice of lemon.

Poland is most famous for its dry herbal vodkas. Many wild plants of Central Europe are featured in their own flavoured vodka, such as *piołunówka* (wormwood) and *dzięgielówka* (angelica), or in recipes that combine many herbs and spices together, such as the bittersweet digestive *żołądkowa gorzka* (containing orange peel, wormwood and cinnamon among many others).

The most famous of all is Poland's pale green *żubrówka*, 'bison vodka'. It is an infusion of vanilla grass, known in Poland as 'bison grass', giving this unusual drink its unusual name. Although the grass grows wild across the entire northern hemisphere, aficionados claim that only the variety grown in the swampy meadows of the Białowieska Forest, where European bison still roam freely, has just the right flavour to make a proper *żubrówka*. The grass (and the alcohol made from it) naturally contains small amounts of coumarin, a flavourful chemical which acts as a blood-thinner and which has been banned by the USA and other countries for use in food and drinks. Special 'coumarin-free' versions are available for export.

Żubrówka is often mixed with apple juice to make a cocktail sometimes called 'Szarlotka' (apple pie) and

sometimes 'Tatanka' (Lakot Sioux for 'buffalo' as well as appearing in the Hollywood film, *Dances with Wolves*). Another local treat is Starka, an aged vodka (technically, a single-grain whiskey) which comes in gradations of quality from 5-year quickies up to the rare, woodsy 50-year Starka.

Whichever vodkas you choose to explore, remember that in Poland you are not required to gulp down your vodka in a single shot. Sipping shows respect for the tipple. Before you drink your vodka, clink your glasses together while looking each other in the eye and say '*na zdrowie!*'

Opposite: Flavoured vodkas for every taste await the adventurous
Above: With over 300 varieties, a night of taste-testing can be quite exhausting!

Hotels and Accommodation

'Balzac slept here', a plaque on one Krakow hotel proudly proclaims. In point of fact, he slept in an entirely different hotel (which no longer exists) with a similar name. Balzac, by the way, was one of the few visitors unimpressed by Krakow. 'A corpse of a capital,' he declared.

There are an increasing number of options available

Prices

Krakow's stormy hotel market has seen a dramatic increase in the number of rooms available as well as overall quality. However, price is not always a good indicator of quality. Some expensive hotels are warmed-over communist eyesores while excellent bargains can be had at the cheap end of the scale.

The Polish star system is an enigma to travellers, based on criteria largely unrelated to the guest's experience of quality. You can safely ignore it entirely.

The following system (unrelated to the Polish star system) is an indication of what one might expect to pay for a double hotel room with toilet and shower in Krakow at the time of writing. Breakfast is usually included. Some hotels may list their prices in euros or dollars but charge in złoty (at their own exchange rate).

★ up to zł69
★★ zł70 to 199
★★★ zł200 to 349
★★★★ zł350 to 599
★★★★★ zł600 or above

Little old ladies lurking near the railway station will offer rooms to anyone who looks like a visitor. Quality and prices of their wares vary from the fantastic to the mediocre. Make sure that you know where the rooms being offered are on the map. In the summer, the many student halls of residence transform themselves into cheap hotels.

Modern hotels have world-class facilities

There are several international chains in Krakow

Location

Most of the hotels on and around Rynek Główny are expensive but there are exceptions. Motels, camping sites, student halls of residence and youth hostels tend to be on the periphery of Krakow. Do not trust a hotel's claim of 'central location' (they may be in the 'central' district but it covers nearly all of urban Krakow): look them up on a map.

Booking

For additional information about hotels in Krakow, consult the comprehensive, bimonthly periodical *Krakow in Your Pocket*, available at the railway station, airport and many newsagents (*www.inyourpocket.com*). Websites like *www.hotelspoland.com* and

www.polhotels.com are also helpful but they do not usually have complete listings. Alternatively try *www.travelpoland.com*, the only professional travel portal in Poland with online hotel reservations. Travelpoland.com is recognised by the Polish Travel Association.

Booking during the summer tourist season (especially at weekends) can be complicated by large tour groups block-booking the larger hotels. Just keep looking, especially at smaller hotels.

Boutique Luxury Hotels

The fanciest hotels in Krakow are *kamienice* (*see p62*), which have been renovated with all the newest conveniences without losing their old-fashioned charm. Staying in one of these can be an experience in itself. Among the best are **Copernicus ★★★★★** (*tel: (012) 424 3400*) and **Wentzl ★★★★★** (*tel: (012) 430 2664*).

International Network Hotels

A number of shiny, clean new hotels have recently been built by international chains and more are expected to open in the next few years. They may not have all the charm of the boutique hotels but they can boast world-class standards. **Ibis Kraków Centrum ★★** (*tel: (012) 299 3300*) and the interestingly-designed **Holiday Inn, City Centre ★★★★★** (*tel: (012) 619 0000*) are good examples of the type. The newest addition is the **Radisson** (*tel: (012) 618 8888*) right next to the Philharmonic and the **Sheraton Krakow** (*tel: (012) 662 1000*).

Traditional Hotels

The backbone of Krakow hotels is still

medium-sized traditional hotels. Some are in Old Town, like: **Francuski** ★★★★★ (*tel: (012) 422 5122*), **Pod Różą** ★★★★ (*tel: (012) 424 3300*), **Pollera** ★★★ (*tel: (012) 422 1044*) and **Saski** ★★★ (*tel: (012) 421 4222*). Kazimierz has a few new hotels that do a good job of reproducing the feel of a traditional hotel, such as **Eden** ★★★ (*tel: (012) 430 6565*) which hosts the only kosher restaurant and *mikveh* (Jewish ritual baths) in Krakow and the charming Jewish-themed **Klezmer Hois** ★★★ (*tel: (012) 411 1245*).

Pensions/Small Hotels

There are many small hotels and *pensions* available in the Krakow area across a wide range of prices and offering a variety of features. Two often overlooked options are the humble but comfortable 'professors' hotels' of the Jagiellonian University: **Dom Gościnny UJ** ★★★ (*tel: (012) 421 1225*) right on

Well-heeled luxury awaits at Sheraton Krakow

The lift at the Saski Hotel

ul. Floriańska and **Bursa im. St. Pigonia** ✦✦✦ (*tel: (012) 422 3008*) overlooking the Carmelite orchard.

Seasonal Hotels
In the summer, visitors are often accosted at the railway station with offers from dormitories that have temporarily become hotels. Some will transport you and your bags to the hotel from the station but **Bratniak** ✦ (*tel: (012) 422 6100*) is the most central.

Hostels and Guestrooms
Cybulskiego Guestrooms
Cybulskiego 6, Krakow. Tel: (012) 423 0532.

Trzy Kafki BIS (Hostel)
Kalwaryjska 42, Krakow. Tel: (012) 263 2010.

Youth Hostels
A younger crowd frequent youth hostels in Poland than elsewhere and their strict curfews will seem insulting to adults. Those who like to share their personal space with pent-up teenagers can try **Oleandry YHA Hostel** ✦ (*tel: (012) 633 8822*) and bring their own sheets.

Apartments and Rooms
An increasingly popular option, especially for those staying a week or more, is to rent a room or flat. **B&B Kraków** (*tel: (012) 623 7791; www.lanierbb.com*) has a wide selection of such places, as do **Old Town Apartments** (*tel: (022) 887 9800; www.warsawhotels.com*) based outside Warsaw.

Camping
For information contact:
Krak
About as upmarket as Krakow's campsites get. Places for tents and caravans with reasonable access to public transport. Very cheap.
ul. Radzikowskiego 99. Tel: (012) 637 2122 ext 106.
Krakowianka
Woody surroundings and a nearby pool. Places in chalets as well as for tents and caravans. Reasonable access to public transport. Very cheap.
ul. Żywiecka Boczna.
Tel: (012) 268 1135, 266 4192, 268 1417.

On Business

Although business boomed in Warsaw in the 1990s, Krakow's business community is growing more slowly. Krakow's proximity to coal- and factory-rich Silesia has led to a little petrochemical business. The vast natural resource of Krakow's 140,000 students, however, has brought in a growing number of cutting-edge enterprises like business outsourcing and software development.

Copying services are plentiful

Business Hours

Many offices open at 9am and close at 5pm, Monday to Friday. Government and university offices often keep shorter hours (10am to 3pm) but they may be open for one Saturday per month. Some offices have complicated systems of accepting petitioners at different times on different days. Banks are usually open from 8am to 5pm, Monday to Saturday.

A stockbroker in Krakow

Conference Centres and Trade Fairs

Two companies specialise in fairs in Krakow. Contact Targi w Krakowie (*tel: (012) 644 5932, 644 8165; fax: (012) 644 6141. www.targi.krakow.pl. e-mail: biuro@targi.krakow.pl*) or Centrum Targowe Chemobudowa Kraków (*tel: (012) 652 7800; fax: (012) 652 7803, 652 7807. www.centrumtargowe.com.pl. e-mail: biuro@centrumtargowe.com.pl*). Most hotels also offer conference venues.

Etiquette

Poles use the formal *Pan* (Mr/sir) or *Pani* (Ms/ma'am) when addressing strangers or business partners. Cracovians are additionally infamous for their attention to proper titles. A male editor would be addressed as *Panie redaktorze* and a female university professor would be *Pani profesor* even outside work. Poland's business community is very conservative about men's suits (usually dark, three-piece) and casual wear on 'dress-down day' is an alien concept.

It is common for men to shake hands at the start of every business day. Men often kiss women's hands, although only if the woman offers her hand first – and the man should bow to her hand, not pull her hand up. Always say *smacznego* (like *bon appetit*) before sharing a meal.

Money

The Polish złoty is fully convertible and is the only legal tender in Poland. Although some hotels and car hires list their prices in dollars or euros, you will still need to pay in złoty.

The *Warsaw Business Journal* is a weekly newspaper in English that is commerce-orientated and gives current exchange rates.

Secretarial, Human Resources and Recruitment Services

Krakow's abundant supply of highly-educated graduates makes HR a buyer's market. Most recruitment services are able to supply both long- and short-term employees. Try Adecco Poland (*tel: (012) 430 0278, 421 2496, 421 2181; fax: (012) 422 1945. e-mail adecco@krakow.adecco.pl*) or Sedlak & Sedlak Personnel Consulting (*tel: (012) 625 5910; fax: (012) 625 5920. e-mail:sedlak@sedlak.com.pl*).

Translation and Interpreting

A wide variety of services, from *tłumaczenia przysięgłe* (sworn translation) to *tłumaczenia symultaniczne* (simultaneous translation), is available from Krakow's many translators. You might try Letterman (*ul. Kremerowska 15/2. Tel: (012) 632 8943; fax: 633 0085*) or

PRO-FIL (*ul. Bartnicka 44, Libertów k. Krakowa. Tel/fax: (012) 270 3281. e-mail: aleksander@idea.net.pl*).

Telefax/Telegram/Telephone

There are telephone centres at both the Main Post Office (*ul. Westerplatte 20*) and the branch by the railway station (*ul. Lubicz 4*) that are open 24 hours a day. The Main Post Office has a telegrams and fax desk (*tel: (012) 421 9693. Open: 7am–9pm*).

Telekomunikacja Polska SA (the national carrier) has a centre with telephone, fax and internet access (no telegrams) at Rynek Główny 19 (*open: Mon–Fri 8am–2am, Sat and Sun 10am–10pm*).

Courier

International courier services (especially across Europe): try DHL (*tel: (0801) 345 345*). Local (inside Poland) courier services: try Stolica (*tel: (012) 638 1600; fax: 638 4388*).

Photocopying

Krakow's many photocopying services range from dirt-cheap to full-service. One of the most comprehensive near the centre is Studio Q (*ul. Karmelicka 18. Tel: (012) 292 7007; fax: 422 3392*).

Office Supplies

Stationery boutiques tend to cluster in Old Town. There are a few larger office supplies stores near the centre like Firma Abc (*ul. Zabłocie 20/22. Tel: (012) 656 5698*) and international behemoths like Office Depot (*ul. Zakopiańska 62. Tel: (012) 261 3130*) in shopping centres on the edges of town.

Practical Guide

Arriving
Formalities
A valid passport is required for entry to Poland, including those arriving from EU countries. Citizens of many countries may enter Poland and stay for 90 days without a visa. Travellers from the UK may stay for 180 days. Travellers from Australia, Canada, Japan, New Zealand and South Africa will need a visa (obtained in the country that issued their passport).

By Air
Krakow's small international airport, named after Pope John Paul II, is in Balice, 18km (11 miles) west of the city. The Nos. 208 and 192 city buses run between the centre and the airport. The airport has public telephones, car rental desks and an accommodation desk.

The first stop for many visitors is the main railway station

The airport has daily flights to and from London, Frankfurt, Zurich, Vienna, New York and Chicago and other destinations are connected by domestic flights via Warsaw.

By Road
Poland has border crossings with Germany, the Czech Republic, Slovakia, Ukraine, Belarus, Lithuania and the Kaliningrad enclave of the Russian Federation. All crossings on major roads are open 24 hours a day. Except for a modern toll road from Katowice, the major roads to and from Krakow are notoriously underdeveloped for their current loads.

By Rail
Krakow's primary international and domestic connection is still the railway. There are quick, easy and cheap connections to many cities throughout Central Europe. All international trains and most domestic trains stop in Kraków Główny station.

Timetables of Polish national and international services can be found in the Thomas Cook European Timetable, updated monthly and available from branches of Thomas Cook in the UK, by telephoning *+44 (1733) 416477*, or buy online from *www.thomascookpublishing.com*. A reliable internet timetable is available (*www.pkp.pl* and look for the link to the English version) but use each country's spelling of its own name.

Children

Children under the age of four ride on municipal public transport free. Children under the age of seven may use *ulgowy* (reduced fare) tickets. Krakow has two children's hospitals: Samodzielny Publiczny Dziecięcy Szpital Kliniczny CM UJ (*ul. Wielicka 265. Tel: (012) 658 2011; fax: 658 1081*) and Wojewódzki Specjalistyczny Szpital Dziecięcy (*ul. Strzelecka 2/4. Tel: (012) 421 1656, 421 1344, 421 1351*).

Climate

(*See pp8–9.*)

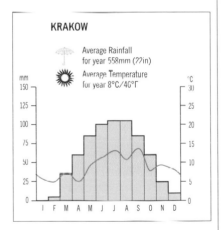

WEATHER CONVERSION CHART

25.4mm = 1 inch

°F = 1.8 × °C + 32

Conversion Tables

Clothes and shoe sizes in Poland follow the standard sizes used in the Rest of Europe.

Conversion Table

FROM	TO	MULTIPLY BY
Inches	Centimetres	2.54
Feet	Metres	0.3048
Yards	Metres	0.9144
Miles	Kilometres	1.6090
Acres	Hectares	0.4047
Gallons	Litres	4.5460
Ounces	Grams	28.35
Pounds	Grams	453.6
Pounds	Kilograms	0.4536
Tons	Tonnes	1.0160

To convert back, for example from centimetres to inches, divide by the number in the third column.

Men's Suits

UK	36	38	40	42	44	46	48
Rest of Europe	46	48	50	52	54	56	58
US	36	38	40	42	44	46	48

Dress Sizes

UK		8	10	12	14	16	18
France		36	38	40	42	44	46
Italy		38	40	42	44	46	48
Rest of Europe		34	36	38	40	42	44
US		6	8	10	12	14	16

Men's Shirts

UK	14	14.5	15	15.5	16	16.5	17
Rest of Europe	36	37	38	39/40	41	42	43
US	14	14.5	15	15.5	16	16.5	17

Men's Shoes

UK	7	7.5	8.5	9.5	10.5	11
Rest of Europe	41	42	43	44	45	46
US	8	8.5	9.5	10.5	11.5	12

Women's Shoes

UK	4.5	5	5.5	6	6.5	7
Rest of Europe	38	38	39	39	40	41
US	6	6.5	7	7.5	8	8.5

Crime

Economic crime (pickpocketing, thefts from hotel rooms, car theft, etc.) is fairly common in Poland but physical violence against foreigners is very rare. Unattended bags and cameras in cafés and bars are particularly popular targets. The railway station and the famous tourist sites are attractive hunting grounds for thieves.

Keep a photocopy of your passport and credit-card information (but not your PIN) handy in a separate location. Thefts that occur anywhere in Old Town or Kazimierz should be reported to the police station at *ul. Szeroka 35 (tel: (012) 422 4535)*. The emergency number for police anywhere in Poland is *997*.

Customs Regulations

Poland is part of the EU, so there are no restrictions on the movement of duty-paid goods for personal use between Poland and other EU countries (except for cigarettes, which are limited to 200 per person).

The allowances for goods bought in duty-free shops (in airports or on board ships and planes), sold free of customs duty and VAT, apply to anyone visiting Poland from a country outside the EU. The allowances here are (per person aged over 17): 200 cigarettes or 100 cigarillos or 50 cigars or 250 gms of tobacco; 1 litre of spirits or 2 litres of table wine, and 2 litres of fortified or sparkling wine; 75cc of perfume.

> **WARNING:** You may not take antiques – meaning anything made before **1945** – out of Poland, no matter where they were produced, without special permits. This includes not just art and printed materials, but anything pre-1945.

Driving

Driving in Krakow is not advised. The streets are narrow and often in bad repair (or under repair). The tangle of one-way and permit-only streets is baffling even to the locals, let alone visitors. Out-of-town

drivers are frequently pulled over by the police, usually by waving a little red reflector on the end of a stick (affectionately known as 'the lollipop'). Many drivers find it easier to park their vehicle safely somewhere on the outskirts and take public transport into town.

Parking

There is no parking actually in the Old Town centre (zone A). Car parks are rare near the centre. Try Plac Szczepański or behind Pałac Pugetów (*ul. Starowiślna 13*). Some hotels may have some parking facilities. Most parking spaces on the narrow streets in and near Old Town are reserved for local residents (zone B). Some streets just outside Old Town (zone C) allow parking with a ticket purchased from an attendant or a kiosk (which needs to have information filled in and be placed prominently under your windscreen) or by paying into coin-operated meters. If you earn a yellow clamp by parking illegally, you should call the number listed on the back of the ticket and an officer will usually show up shortly to tell you how much you must pay.

Breakdown

If your vehicle breaks down in a public place, a surprising number of private repair services will rush to the scene. If help has not already arrived, try calling Pomoc Drogowa (breakdown service) on *tel: 981*. They are not likely to speak English but if you can tell them what street or road you are on, they will understand. It is advisable to have comprehensive insurance to cover all eventualities and repatriation to your home country.

Car Hire

Different companies will have different minimum ages for car hire. Most companies require the foreign hirer to present a passport and driving licence as well as possess a credit card or leave a hefty deposit. Many travellers find that it is cheaper and easier to arrange car hire through their airline. The usual international networks like Avis (*tel: (012) 629 6108*) and Hertz (*tel: (012) 429 6262*) are here as well as local competitors like Joka (*tel: (012) 429 6630*). A hefty slice of the cost of hiring a car is VAT (value-added tax).

Most companies will not require you to pay for insurance as long as you agree to let them charge your credit card for any damage. 'Promotions' on buying their insurance together with hiring their car are usually geared to make the total cost come out nearly the same whether you buy insurance or not.

Documents and Insurance

Most foreign licences are accepted for periods up to six months after arrival but an International Driving Licence is recommended. You will need to keep the vehicle registration document handy. New registration plates from EU member countries already display the vehicle's country identification but non-EU registered vehicles will need an additional sticker. You are expected to carry a fire extinguisher, with a sticker proving current validity, and a red warning triangle in your vehicle. A first-aid kit is recommended.

Fuel

Benzyna (petrol) is usually available in 94 and 95 octane leaded and 94, 95 and 98 unleaded. Diesel is more commonly known these days by its English name than the Polish *olej napędowy*. There are very few petrol stations anywhere near the city centre of Krakow, but there are many of them as soon as you head towards the outskirts in any direction. There are international chains like **BP** as well as local suppliers like **Orlen**. Many petrol stations also have small convenience stores, some of which may be open on national holidays.

Traffic Regulations

Drive on the right. Seatbelts are obligatory, although this is rarely enforced for passengers in the back seats. Children under 12 years of age must travel in a child seat unless they are taller than 150cm (4ft 11in). Do not drive under the influence of alcohol. Trams have the right of way – be alert when crossing tram tracks. Overtaking trams is forbidden when the tram is at a passenger stop – there will be people getting on and off.

Many major streets and bridges have the right-hand lane reserved for buses and taxis during rush hour. Many streets in and around Old Town are one-way or have restricted turns. Passenger vehicles may not enter the A zone of Krakow. Passenger vehicles may not normally enter the B zone of Krakow without a permit – which travellers will not be able to get. If your hotel is in the B zone and has a car park, you are allowed exactly 15 minutes there before you are in violation. You may drive in the C zone, but parking is usually restricted. The zones are marked on signposts.

Speed limits are usually 110kph (68.5mph) on motorways, less in more built-up areas. Road signs follow European norms. All accidents must be reported to the police (*tel: 997*).

Electricity
220 volts, 50 cycle AC. Standard continental adaptors are suitable. Visitors requiring 110 volts will need a voltage transformer. Many laptop computer power supplies are capable of running on more than one voltage (read your power supply's voltage requirements carefully before experimenting).

Embassies and Consulates
Australia
The nearest is the Embassy in Warsaw (*tel: (022) 521 3444*).
Canada
The nearest is the Embassy in Warsaw (*tel: (022) 584 3100*).
Ireland
The nearest is the Embassy in Warsaw (*tel: (022) 849 6655*).
New Zealand
The nearest is the Embassy in Bonn, Germany (*tel: +49 (228) 228 070*).
UK
Consulate, *ul. św. Anny 9* (*tel: (012) 421 7030*).
USA
Consulate, *ul. Stolarska 9* (*tel: (012) 429 6655*).

Emergency Telephone Numbers
Ambulance *999*
Chemist (Pharmacy) Open 24 hours a day, inside the Tesco hypermarket (*ul. Kapelanka 56. Tel: (012) 296 4239*).
Fire brigade *998*
Police *997*

Health
By the terms of bilateral agreements, citizens of the UK, Sweden and Slovakia are granted free medical care in Poland. Travellers from most other countries are expected to pay for medical services. In theory, you should apply to the nearest *przychodnia* (walk-in clinic) with your non-emergency problems. There is a central one on *Pl. Świętego Ducha 3 (tel: (012) 422 1771)*. However, the bureaucracy that travellers must negotiate to get to a public doctor can be daunting. Medicover (*ul. Krótka 1. Tel: 430 0034. www.medicover.pl*) offers English-speaking doctors and staff at a private clinic at international prices. For emergency services, call for an ambulance on *tel: **999***.

Insurance
You should take out personal travel insurance. It should give adequate cover for medical expenses, loss, theft, repatriation, personal liability, third-party motor insurance (but liability arising from motor accidents is not usually included) and cancellation expenses.

If you will be travelling in your own vehicle, check with your insurers about cover for damage, loss or theft of the vehicle as well as liability. A Green Card is recommended to avoid paying additional insurance at the border.

Internet
Many hotels in Krakow offer in-room internet connections and internet cafés are ubiquitous. One of the most popular with foreign visitors is U Louisa (*Rynek Główny 13. Tel: (012) 431 1822*) which has lots of Old Town atmosphere.

Lost Property

Apply to Biuro Rzeczy Znalezionych at *Al. Powstania Warszawskiego 10, fifth floor, room 504 (tel: (012) 616 9289).*

Maps

Tourist information offices (*see p189*) and many hotels give out free maps of the city centre. For outlying districts, you will do better with a *plan miasta* (city map) purchased at any newsagent.

Media

All English-language newspapers in Poland are based in Warsaw and are rarely seen in Krakow. Fortunately, major international titles like the *Financial Times*, the *International Herald Tribune* and *The Economist* are available at many newsagents in the city centre, often with a one-day delay. EMPiK on *Rynek Główny 5 (tel: (012) 429 4577. www.empik.pl)* tends to have the best selection (downstairs for general news, upstairs for more specialised titles). Most hotels have access to international news broadcasts like BBC World, Sky News and CNN.

Money Matters

The Polish unit of currency is the *złoty* (abbreviated to 'zł' with the code PLN at currency exchanges). It is divided into 100 units called *groszy* in denominations of 1, 2, 5, 10, 20 and 50gr coins. There are also zł1, 2 and 5 coins, as well as zł10, 20, 50, 100 and 200 notes. Shops and other services are often unable to give change for large notes in the morning. You will frequently be asked for near-exact money when making any purchase, even if the cashier has a full till.

Currency exchanges, under the 'kantor' sign, may be found all over Old Town

Changing Money

Usual banking hours are 8am–5pm, Monday to Saturday. Shop around the exchange offices on Floriańska and Szewska for the best deal. The cashpoint (ATM) machines usually offer a good exchange rate on money withdrawn from foreign accounts.

Neither traveller's cheques nor personal cheques are accepted in lieu of cash anywhere in Krakow. Currency exchanges will not cash them and some banks will inflict long queues, tiresome bureaucracy and even waiting periods before you can get your money. The only convenient place to cash a traveller's cheque is the Małopolskie Centrum Informacji Turystycznej (the Małopolska Tourist Information Centre) on the outside of the Sukiennice, near the Mariacki church, *Rynek Główny 1/3 (tel: (012) 421 7706, 421 3051).*

LANGUAGE

Polish has a complicated grammar and a rich selection of sounds that do not exist in English. Fortunately, most younger people speak some English and older generations will usually know German or French.

PRONUNCIATION

The stress is always on the penultimate syllable of a word.

Vowel Sounds

a like an English 'a' in 'f**a**ther'

ą sometimes like a French 'on' as in 'm**on**', sometimes like an English 'on' as in 'g**on**e' and sometimes like an English 'om' as in 'T**om**'

e as in 'g**e**t'

ę sometimes like a French 'in' as in 'v**in**', sometimes like an English 'en' as in '**en**d' and sometimes like an English 'em' as in '**em**bark'

i like an English 'ee' as in 's**ee**'

o as in 'sl**o**w'

ó and **u** like an English 'oo' as in 'c**oo**l'

y as in 'm**y**sterious'

Consonants

b, f, g, k, m, n, p and **w** if followed by **i** are pronounced as if they were the consonant followed by a 'y' as in 'yell', for example, **ki** like the 'ky' in jun**ky**ard

c like 'ts' in 'ca**ts**'

ch and **h** a harsher 'h' at the back of the throat

cz like 'ch' in 'su**ch**' but with the tongue further back

ć or **ci** like 'tch' in 'i**tch**' with the tongue forward

ż like 'j' in '**j**ump' but with the tongue further back

dź and **dzi** like the 'j' in '**j**ar' with the tongue forward

NUMBERS

1	jeden (but *raz* when counting)
2	dwa
3	trzy
4	cztery
5	pięć
6	sześć
7	siedem
8	osiem
9	dziewięć
10	dziesięć
20	dwadzieścia
100	sto (plural = setki)

g always hard as in 'get'

j like 'y' in '**y**ell'

ł like 'w' in '**w**in'

ń like a Spanish 'ñ' in 'se**ñ**ior'

r rolled like Spanish or Russian

rz similar to the 's' in 'mea**s**ure'

sz similar to the 'sh' in 'ru**sh**' but with the tongue further back

ś and **si** like the 'sh' in 'fi**sh**' with the tongue forward

w like the 'v' in '**v**isit'

ż and **zi** similar to the 's' in 'mea**s**ure'

ź similar to the 's' in 'mea**s**ure' but with the tongue further back

BASIC PHRASES

yes	tak
no	nie
please/	proszę
you're welcome	
thank you	dziękuję
bon appetit	smacznego
hi/bye	cześć (informal)
hello/good day	dzień dobry (formal)
goodbye	do widzenia
good evening	dobry wieczór
good night	dobranoc
excuse me	przepraszam
I don't understand	nie rozumiem
where?	gdzie?
when?	kiedy?
why?	dlaczego?
how much?	ile?
expensive	drogi
cheap	tani
small	mały
large	duży
open	otwarty
closed	zamknięty
quickly	szybko
slowly	wolno
cold	zimny
hot	gorący
to the left	w lewo
to the right	w prawo
straight ahead	prosto
near	blisko
far	daleko
day	dzień
week	tydzień
month	miesiąc
year	rok
food	jedzenie
drink	picie
water	woda
wine	wino
menu	menu
bath	wanna

shower	prysznic
medical doctor	lekarz
thief	zlodziej
police	policja
currency exchange	kantor
bus	autobus
tram	tramwaj
taxi	taksówka
still water	woda niegazowana
beer	piwo
vodka	wódka
cigarettes	papierosy

DAYS OF THE WEEK

Sunday	niedziela
Monday	poniedziałek
Tuesday	wtorek
Wednesday	środa
Thursday	czwartek
Friday	piątek
Saturday	sobota

Do you speak English? To a man (formal):
Czy pan mówię po angielsku?

Do you speak English? To a woman (formal):
Czy pani mówię po angielsku?

I do not speak Polish
Nie mówię po polsku

I do not understand
Nie rozumiem

Does someone speak English here?
Czy ktoś tu mówię po angielsku?

Please speak slowly
Prosze mówię powoli

Where is Wawel?
Gdzie jest Wawel?

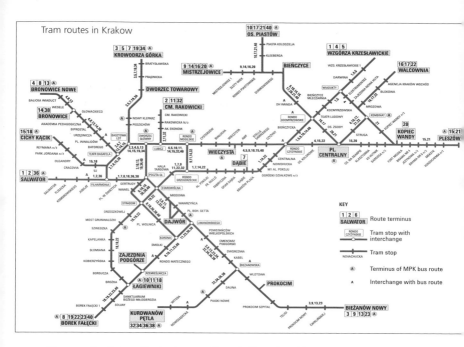

Tram routes in Krakow

Thomas Cook traveller's cheques free you from the hazards of carrying large amounts of cash and, in the event of loss or theft, can be quickly refunded. Thomas Cook Traveller's Cheque Refund: 24-hour service – report loss or theft within 24 hours (*tel: +44 1733 318950; see pp188–9 for information about how to reverse charges*).

Credit Cards
Credit cards can be used in most restaurants and larger or upmarket shops. They are not commonly used in bars or cafés. They can even be used to pay for train tickets and some taxi fares (the credit card logo will be posted on the window). You can receive cash advances on your credit cards from most cashpoint (ATM) machines.

Opening Hours
Stores and Shops
Many shops are open 10am–6pm, Monday to Friday, and 10am–3pm (or earlier) on Saturday. Food shops usually keep slightly longer hours and some are open on Sunday. The international hypermarket Tesco (*ul. Kapelanka 54*) is open 24 hours a day. Many shops are closed for longer periods around Christmas and New Year and from Good Friday to Easter Monday.

Galleries and Museums
Most museums are closed on Mondays and national holidays. They tend to have complicated schedules with different opening times on different days but often fall around 10am–4pm, Tuesday to Sunday. A few museums are open on

Polish national holidays but closed on what would normally be a working day in the same month to compensate.

Police

Look for Policja (the regular Polish Police) or Straż Miejska (the Krakow Town Guard). Although there is a small police station on Rynek Główny, the main headquarters for Old Town is in an unassuming building down in Kazimierz (*ul. Szeroka 35. Tel: (012) 422 2081*).

Post Offices

The Main Post Office is at *ul. Westerplatte 20, 31-045 Krakow (tel: (012) 422 4811. Open: Mon–Fri 7.30am–10.30pm, Sat 8am–2pm, Sun 9am–2pm).* Stamps and phone cards can be purchased here. At least one

queue at most post offices is dedicated to a cashier for paying monthly bills. That queue is usually the longest and the cashier will not be able to sell you stamps or phone cards. Some post offices have an automated system where you take a number from a machine and wait until your number flashes over one of the windows.

Public Holidays

1 January – New Year's Day
Easter Monday – variable
1 May – May Day
3 May – Constitution Day
Corpus Christi – variable
1 November – All Saints Day
11 November – Independence Day
25–26 December – Christmas

Bus routes in Krakow

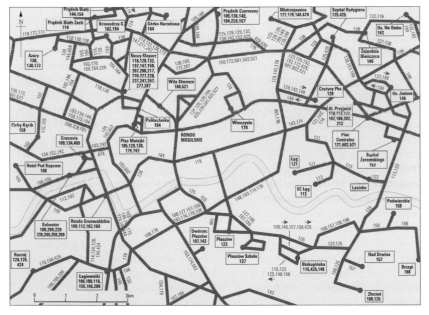

Public Transport

Public transport (*see pp25–6*) is very cheap and efficient. You can buy tickets for a single journey (without transfers) or for a period of time (such as an hour of travel including transfers). Single-journey and short-term tickets may be purchased from all newsagents or from the driver for a small fee. Daily or weekly tickets are a good bargain for visitors. These longer-term tickets may only be purchased directly from the public transport company at one of their kiosks (there are convenient ones on ul. Lubicza near the railway station and on ul. Podwale near where ul. Szewska meets the outer edge of the Planty). The same tickets are good for both trams and buses. Most public transport runs between 5am and 11pm. Night buses run much less frequently and on fewer routes, and are more expensive.

Outside Krakow

The rail network connects Krakow with all of Europe. Most arrivals and departures are from the imperial-yellow, neo-Gothic Kraków Główny station (on Plac Kolejowy). For details and timetables, consult the Thomas Cook European Timetable, which is available from Thomas Cook branches in the UK, by calling *01733 416477*, or buy online at *www.thomascookpublishing.com*

On the opposite side of the square stands the rather shabby-looking Dworzec PKS (bus station), which operates routes throughout Poland and to a few international destinations. Coaches are usually cheaper than trains but less comfortable.

Religious Worship

Roman Catholic mass is held in English at Kościół św. Idziego (St Giles') at the end of ul. Grodzka near Wawel every Sunday at 10.30am. Roman Catholic mass is held in German at Kościół św. Barbary (St Barbara's) behind the Mariacki church every Sunday. Orthodox Jewish services (mostly in Hebrew) are held in Remuh Synagogue. Most other services are in Polish.

Student and Youth Travel

Many student discounts (such as on municipal public transport) are only available to holders of Polish student identification. International student cards (ISIC), available from Almatur (*ul. Grodzka 2. Tel: (012) 422 4668; fax: 428 4520. krakow@almatur.pl*), will work for discounted rail tickets and most museums.

Taxis

The most reliable cab drivers are members of one of the taxi associations, which prominently display the telephone number of the association on the roof and/or sides of the taxi. The most popular are 919, 96-22, 96-25, 96-61, 96-64 and 96-67. You can find them at most taxi ranks or by calling one of the numbers. In Krakow, they will offer you a 10 per cent discount on your fare if you call.

Telephones

Public phones are available in all parts of Krakow, with a large number around Rynek Główny. Phone cards are available in several denominations at newsagents and post offices. There are two different types of cards: chip and magnetic strip.

To make a call to another city inside Poland, dial '0' followed by the two-digit city code and your number. To call Warsaw dial 022, Oświęcim 033, Zakopane 018.

To make a call to another country, dial *00* followed by the country code:

Australia *61*
Canada and USA *1*
New Zealand *64*
UK *44*

Then dial the full number.

To reverse charges on an international call, first call the Country Direct number:

UK: (00 800) 441 1144, 441 1202
USA: (00 800) 111 1111, 111 1112.

Then give the operator the number that you are calling and request reversed charges.

Thomas Cook

Thomas Cook services in Poland are available through Neckermann travel shops. In Krakow there is a branch at the M-1 Shopping Centre on *Aleja Pokoju 67 (tel: (012) 686 1011. Tel/fax: (012) 686 1113. e-mail: krakow,m1@ neckermann.pl).* You cannot cash traveller's cheques at the branch but they will offer emergency assistance.

Time

All of Poland follows Central European Time, which is Greenwich Mean Time +1 hour, or Eastern Standard Time +6 hours. Between March and late September, clocks are advanced 1 hour.

Toilets

Most restaurants and bars will charge 50gr or zł1 for the use of their toilets.

Women's toilets are usually marked with a circle or sometimes '**damskie**'; men's with a triangle or sometimes '**męskie**'. It is not a bad idea to keep a small supply of toilet paper or facial tissues on your person in case there are not any provided.

Tourist Information

The Culture Information Centre on *ul. Jana 2 (tel: (012) 421 7787; fax: 421 7731)* always has the best information on festivals, classical music, art galleries and other 'high' art. They can sell you tickets to some events and publish a very cheap, pocket-sized monthly 'Karnet'. The Tourist Information Centre in the Planty park (*near ul. Szpitalna. Tel: (012) 432 0060, 432 0110*) is more geared towards hotels and excursions. The Małopolskie Centrum Informacji Turystycznej (the Małopolska Tourist Information Centre) on the outside of the Sukiennice, near the Mariacki church (*Rynek Główny 1/3. Tel: (012) 421 7706, 421 3051*) has a cashier's desk that can cash traveller's cheques, and a selection of tourist guides and albums. Many things marked as 'tourist information' in Krakow are, in fact, branches of travel shops or insurance agents.

Travellers with Disabilities

Although the situation is improving by the day, very little of Krakow is disability-friendly and even less is prepared for non-Polish-speaking foreigners with disabilities. The principal tourist sights will usually have a wheelchair ramp.

ACKNOWLEDGEMENTS

Thomas Cook Publishing wishes to thank the photographers and other organisations for the loan of the photographs reproduced in this book, to whom the copyright in the photographs belong.

view with a grain of sand, Wisława Szymborska. Front cover reproduced with kind permission of Harcourt Brace, page 23.

CHRISTOPHER HOLT pages 1, 2, 4, 5, 9, 10, 11, 12, 13, 17, 18a, 19, 20a, 21, 24b, 28, 31, 32b, 33, 36, 37, 39, 40b, 43, 45, 47, 51, 52, 54, 56, 57, 60, 61, 72, 73, 74, 75, 78, 80b, 82, 83, 84, 85, 87, 92b, 93b, 94, 95, 98, 106a, 107, 110, 113, 114, 115, 117, 118, 122, 124b, 126, 127, 129, 130b, 134a, 135a, 140, 142, 146, 147a, 149, 151, 152, 156, 158, 161, 163, 164, 167, 172a, 172b, 174, 176a, 178 and 183.

SIMON CYGIELSKI pages 6, 8, 14, 15, 16, 18b, 20b, 22, 24a, 26, 27, 29, 30, 32a, 34, 35, 38, 40a, 41, 44, 46, 50, 55, 62, 63, 64, 65, 66, 67, 68, 69, 76, 77, 79, 80a, 81, 86, 89, 90, 92a, 93a, 96, 97, 99, 100, 101, 102, 103, 105, 106b, 108, 109, 111, 116, 119, 121, 123, 124a, 125, 130a, 131, 133, 134b, 135b, 136, 138, 139, 141, 143, 144, 147b, 148, 150a, 150b, 157, 159a, 159b, 160, 165, 166, 168, 169, 170, 171, 173, 175 and 176b.

Index: Indexing Specialists (UK) Ltd

Maps: IFA Design Ltd, Plymouth, UK

Proof-reading: JOANNE OSBORN for Cambridge Publishing Management Ltd

Send your thoughts to
books@thomascook.com

We're committed to providing the very best up-to-date information in our travel guides and constantly strive to make them as useful as they can be. You can help us to improve future editions by letting us have your feedback. If you've made a wonderful discovery on your travels that we don't already feature, if you'd like to inform us about recent changes to anything that we do include, or if you simply want to let us know your thoughts about this guidebook and how we can make it even better – we'd love to hear from you.

Send us ideas, discoveries and recommendations today and then look out for your valuable input in the next edition of this title. And, as an extra 'thank you' from Thomas Cook Publishing, you'll be automatically entered into our exciting monthly prize draw.

Emails to the above address, or letters to Travellers Project Editor, Thomas Cook Publishing, PO Box 227, Units 15–16, Coningsby Road, Peterborough PE3 8SB, UK.

Please don't forget to let us know which title your feedback refers to!